STICKS
and
STONES

Other Books by Ace Collins

Turn Your Radio On:
The Stories behind Gospel Music's
All-Time Greatest Songs

The Cathedrals:
The Story of America's
Best-Loved Gospel Quartet

Stories behind the Best-Loved
Songs of Christmas

Stories behind the Hymns
That Inspire America

Stories behind the Great
Traditions of Christmas

I Saw Him in Your Eyes:
Everyday People Making
Extraordinary Impact

More Stories behind the Best-Loved
Songs of Christmas

Stories behind the Traditions and
Songs of Easter

Stories behind Women of
Extraordinary Faith

Farraday Road

STICKS and STONES

USING YOUR WORDS as a POSITIVE FORCE

ACE COLLINS

ZONDERVAN®

ZONDERVAN.com/
AUTHORTRACKER
follow your favorite authors

We want to hear from you. Please send your comments about this book to us in care of zreview@zondervan.com. Thank you.

ZONDERVAN

Sticks and Stones
Copyright © 2009 by Andrew Collins

This title is also available in a Zondervan audio edition.
Visit www.zondervan.fm.

Requests for information should be addressed to:

Zondervan, *Grand Rapids, Michigan 49530*

Library of Congress Cataloging-in-Publication Data

Collins, Ace.
     Sticks and stones : using your words as a positive force / Ace Collins.
        p.   cm.
     ISBN 978-0-310-28253-2 (hardcover)
      1. Interpersonal communication. 2. Communication — Psychological aspects.
   3. Interpersonal relations. I. Title.
   BF637.C45C635 2009
   177'.2 — dc22   2008049808

Any Internet addresses (websites, blogs, etc.) and telephone numbers printed in this book are offered as a resource. They are not intended in any way to be or imply an endorsement by Zondervan, nor does Zondervan vouch for the content of these sites and numbers for the life of this book.

Interior design by Christine Orejuela-Winkelman

Printed in the United States of America

09 10 11 12 13 14 15 • 22 21 20 19 18 17 16 15 14 13 12 11 10 9 8 7 6 5 4 3 2

To Jane,
for her incredible vision
and unique way of sharing it

Contents

Introduction

Words Can Never Harm Me

One of the most familiar of childhood sayings is, "Sticks and stones can break my bones, but words can never harm me." If only that were true! Words have derailed political campaigns, started wars, ruined marriages, and even led to a man named Jesus being crucified on the cross. The fact is, words are a powerful tool and perhaps an even more powerful weapon. They can destroy and they can inspire. And how we use them says a great deal about each of us.

As a writer I have had the privilege of interviewing some of the most incredible people in the world. Their words and stories have made a profound impact on my life. Yet I have not had the opportunity to share many of the lessons I've learned from these experiences with anyone but my family and friends. What I have learned has so changed the way I view the power of words that I felt a need to share these lessons in the very medium that I have come to realize has so much power—a book.

Consider this: Ron Ballard was paralyzed from the neck down after a car wreck. He was confined to a single room in his parents' home. He should have been forgotten, but one Sunday-school teacher's words not only kept him alive but also gave him the faith and drive to start a movement that changed the world for tens of millions of other disabled people.

Or how about this: Gene Mauldin was always told he would amount to nothing. He heard it so much that he believed every word. Only after he was blinded during the Vietnam War did someone finally tell him how much talent he had been given. He took that belief and became an honors student in college and eventually one of St. Louis's top homebuilders. Words allowed him to see his potential even after he lost his sight.

I felt I needed to share these and scores of other stories. Putting this book together became a mission that simply would not let me go. You are holding in your hand the essence of what I believe is a formula for combating an increasingly negative world. In these pages are examples of how thinking before we speak or write can open up new horizons for those around us. And with your positive influence, those you touch will touch others, and the world will become a brighter place. We need that light in this century filled with so many fears and uncertainties.

In his play *Richelieu; Or the Conspiracy*, Edward Bulwer-Lytton wrote the famous line, "The pen is mightier than the sword." How true. When properly used, words, both written and spoken, can make a greater and longer-lasting impact than the most powerful weapons ever constructed. Yet in a time when the average person employs thirty thousand words daily through conversation and correspondence, most of our words miss a great deal more often than they hit, and those that hit often cause pain, not healing.

Properly used, language can and should have a positive impact. Words should cause people to stop, think, and grow. They should bring comfort, cheer, and inspiration. They should change the world by influencing individuals in a positive manner. While what we say or write might never be quoted like Lincoln's "Gettysburg Address" or Paul's love passage in 1 Corinthians 13, with just a little thought and effort, each of us can cause our family, friends, co-workers, and even complete strangers to try to meet their highest goals or to reach down to lift another up.

We live in an era when language is simply tossed about in an unthinking manner or spun to fit an agenda. Though we as individuals talk a great deal in person and on cell phones and, thanks to the internet, write more personal and business notes than any previous generation, we don't as carefully consider our choice of words as did people of earlier times. Most of us, including parents, church leaders, CEOs, coaches, and friends, just "shoot from the hip" and do far more damage with our words than we realize. While a word or phrase more carefully chosen might have inspired someone, what we see much more often today is the use of words that hurt and destroy individuals.

Using real-life examples, this book presents simple ways in which everyone can make a positive impact with their language. Whether it's in conversations, email, letters, phone calls, thank-yous, and even blogging, you will discover ways to employ words that will change the world. There is nothing revolutionary in this book, just written reminders put together in formulas that might help you make words a positive force in what has become a very negative world. If you want to make those thirty thousand words you use each day count, then this book will help you get more out of the time you spend communicating with others each and every day.

1

Talking to Yourself

A few years ago I was watching a high-school girls' basketball game in a small town in Texas. It was an exciting contest, with parents cheering for the kids, coaches yelling out instructions, and players using their talents to try to score points on one end of the gym and stop their opponents on the other.

The point guard for the Bynum Lady Bulldogs was a cute, small brunette named Brittany. The fifteen-year-old was doing her best to bring the ball up the floor against a suffocating full-court press. Moving to her right, Brittany dribbled up the sideline, only to be confronted by a double-team and to have the ball bounced against her knee and out of bounds. After the whistle blew, there was a moment of almost churchlike silence in the building. Then Brittany cried out, "Oh, Brittany!"

Brittany was obviously upset with her play. Her words, meant to be heard by no one other than herself, indicated her frustration even more than the look on her face did. As the game continued, I noted that she continued to whisper words of encouragement and exclamations of frustration to herself for the rest of the night. In fact, I found her one-sided conversation to be the most interesting part of the game.

Like Brittany, we all talk to ourselves. It's part of our nature. Contrary to popular opinion, we aren't crazy just because we ask ourselves questions and then provide a few answers. Many of us might not voice our thoughts, but I don't know of anyone who doesn't internalize conversations. What we say to ourselves varies from day to day and situation to situation, but how we say it affects not only our choices in life but how we relate to the rest of the world. If our own words label us as losers, then we usually live down to that status.

I Think I Can!

One of the best-loved children's stories is about a small locomotive trying to pull a big load up a mountain. While we might not remember the details of the story, the tiny engine's words are probably still etched in everyone's mind: "I think I can, I think I can, I think I can!" Using that philosophy, the tiny locomotive steamed over the mountain and then proudly told itself, "I knew I could!"

For many, though, the voice we hear on the inside more often than not says, "You can't do that." And if those are the words you hear each day, then you probably aren't able to say much that is encouraging to anyone else either.

An old axiom says you really can't like others unless you like yourself. This can be expanded to include another significant rule: you really can't say much to motivate others in a positive way if you are drowning in doubts and negativity.

Picture It Happening

One of the reasons I enjoy watching kids play basketball is that I played all through grade school and high school. In fact, I still like to get out on the court today. In addition, my father was an incredible coach who excelled at teaching fundamental skills. Several of his players went on to play at major colleges.

Dad taught us how to shoot free throws. He went into every nuance, including fingertip control, stance, and release. Yet even though he could teach the proper technique to every kid, certain individuals simply couldn't consistently hit free throws. The problem wasn't with their form; it was in their head. They always went up to the line convinced they were going to miss the shot. They couldn't latch on to my dad's best piece of advice: "Picture it going through the goal before you release the ball." Instead, the picture in their minds was of the ball clanking on the rim and falling off to the side. Rather than having an "I know I can make it" attitude, they said to themselves words like, "I'm going to miss it."

Even when everything is going right in your life, even when you have the skills, the experience, and the tools to accomplish something, if you are telling yourself, "I am going to mess this up," you probably will. The words you speak to yourself are probably the most important words you will ever say.

Breaking the Mold

Several weeks ago I read the story of Nola Ochs. In May 2007 she graduated with honors from Fort Hays State University in Hays, Kansas. As the history major received her degree, everyone, including the governor of the state, stood and applauded. Her blue eyes glowing, the small woman grinned, took her diploma, and moved across the stage and back to her seat. The ever-modest Nola considered herself to be just another student and didn't want to steal the spotlight from any of her many friends in the class of 2007. Yet the fact that she was ninety-five years old did cast her in a much different light than her classmates.

As middle age begins to throw its arms around us, our internal voice tells us to slow down and give up on our dreams. The voice inside our head that once pushed us to try to change the world now screams, "You can't do that now; you are simply too old." This voice usually becomes louder as we hit our senior years. Rather than think with the old "I think I can" mentality, we tend to say, "I wish I could," or even worse, "There's no way."

Nola never allowed her mind to convince her body that she couldn't do anything she dreamed of doing. She had run a large family farm after her husband died. She had driven tractors, bailed hay, and taken crops to the market. She had raised livestock. All the while, the voice in her head kept saying, "You know you can do it." When most members of her high school class were holding their reunions at the cemetery, Nola took some courses at a community college and then at the age of ninety-four moved to the campus at Fort Hays State to become a coed. She donned the colors of the Fort Hays State Tigers at the same time as her granddaughter did.

Nola's work ethic, self-discipline, and drive inspired her professors and other students, who were often seven decades her junior. As they got to know Nola, they were transformed simply by watching her positive approach to life. Her can-do spirit pulled a lot of self-doubters to heights they never believed they could achieve. Students who were tempted to skip classes or put off homework got out of bed and went to work because of the white-haired student who greeted each challenge with a big smile and an even bigger can-do attitude.

One of the keys to Nola's success was very simple; Nola liked herself. She felt she had value and worth. She was confident enough to walk into a situation in which she would stand out, in which most people expected her to fail or fall behind. Each day, she got up believing she could handle whatever life threw at her. She even felt it was a joy to meet those challenges.

Her work ethic, the premium she put on learning, her quest to embrace fully every moment of her life, and her positive attitude made a huge impact on her fellow students. The kids who went to school with her saw firsthand that there was nothing that could hold them back or stand in their way except their own attitudes. When they watched Nola gain her degree, they understood that with hard work and the right can-do spirit, they too could realize the fullness of a life that has no boundaries.

Looking Ahead

For every Nola there are tens of thousands of people of all ages who simply believe they are too old, too short, too slow, too thin, too fat, or just too something to do anything. Hence they don't even start to do what they really want to do. The voice inside their head is a "can't-do attitude." They are constantly explaining to themselves and to others that what they wish for can never be realized because of something that is holding them back. The words they speak to themselves are excuses rather than challenges.

The attitude expressed by the words "I just can't do it" not only holds people back in their own lives but also is passed on to others. If someone close to you has this attitude, it can affect you as deeply as it does them. That can't-do voice is a dead weight pulling down everyone in their sphere of influence.

A Change of Attitude Changes the Way You Speak to Yourself

In 1952, Dr. Norman Vincent Peale wrote a book that became one of the bestselling releases of its time. *The Power of Positive Thinking* addressed, in straightforward language, why attitude is the most important factor in achieving personal happiness. Millions adopted Peale's positive approach to living as part of their lives.

Though it didn't explain it in this fashion, Peale's book is essentially about the way we talk to ourselves. If we are negative, if we spend our lives waiting for something bad to happen, then one of two things will transpire. We will either be confronted by something bad or we will die waiting to have something bad hit us. Neither of these options offers much comfort.

The Dangers of Our Negative Words

Howard Hughes was a genius, a maverick, and a dreamer. His successes in business, aviation, and media made him one of the world's wealthiest and most powerful individuals, but even though he was blessed with incredible riches and was admired by millions, Hughes's attitude doomed him to withdraw from the world.

For decades, hiding behind closed curtains and locked doors, Howard Hughes lived his life in fear, terrified that he was going to get sick and die. Sadly, his fear of death caused him to miss most of the joy of life. His self-concept, the words he spoke to himself, drowned him in a sea of misery. His incredible wealth made his death that much more ironic. Yet though he may have taken it to the extreme, Hughes is just one of millions who tell themselves they have so much to fear that their worries never allow them to fully enjoy a single moment of life.

A Solid Self-View Can Start a Revolution

A good self-concept is vital to making an impact with your words. If you have a positive approach to your life, if you believe in your potential, then others will notice and want to follow you. Even if you don't realize it, you will be a leader.

Throughout the 1930s, Hollywood produced scores of films that featured an underdog overcoming the odds and rising to the top. Nowhere was this more prevalent than in the musicals of the era. In the plot of one musical, an understudy who believed in herself was pushed into the lead part on opening night and proved her worth in front of a theater filled with skeptical patrons. The underlying theme of all of these films, be they musicals or movies about boxers, racehorses, senators, or even John Doe, is that the underdog looked in the mirror and said, "I can do this!"

Hattie McDaniel was an incredibly talented woman who was born a century too early to be fully recognized by her peers. A gifted singer and performer, in the 1930s she turned to acting to pay the rent. With her large figure and expressive face, she was a regular character actress in many of the top films of the decade. Still, the African-American woman seemed doomed to be little more than a background player whose portrayals continued a negative stereotype of her race.

In 1939, Hollywood released what is still considered to be one of the finest films ever made. Based on a bestselling novel, *Gone with the Wind* is four hours of drama, excitement, and history all set in the Old South. The cast assembled for the feature represented a who's who of the industry. As the most-hyped film ever, this was a movie that every A-list actor wanted to be in.

One of the featured parts of this Civil War–era epic was written for a house slave everyone called Mammy. A lot of African-American women auditioned for the role, but the producer, David O. Selznick, sensed that Hattie McDaniel was perfect for the part.

By playing Mammy, McDaniel would make more money in a few months than she had made in all her years of acting. However, it also placed her in the uncomfortable position of playing a slave at the same time African-Americans were beginning to fight to gain equal status. So before signing the contract, Hattie had a talk with herself, then a conversation with the producer. She explained to Selznick that she wanted to play Mammy with dignity, that she wanted this woman to be a three-dimensional character who might be a slave but who still had great strength. Her Mammy would have incredible influence wrapped in an independent spirit. Finally, she wanted the producer to know that she would not say a single line of dialogue that would disparage her race. The risk McDaniel took was huge—she was well aware Selznick could have chosen someone else—but he agreed to her terms. He understood her feelings, and her words drew him to make the changes to accommodate the woman's strong values.

Over the course of the filming, Hattie became one of the favorite members of the cast. The crew loved her, and at a time when race divided everything, she was treated as an equal even to the great Clark Gable. She was anything but a token minority; her attitude made her an equal on the set.

Hattie's portrayal in *Gone with the Wind* reflected her dynamic can-do spirit and transformed Mammy from a background figure to one of the most important characterizations ever to grace a Hollywood film. Because of the way she spoke to herself, and the strength that gave her, when she won an Oscar for her performance, McDaniel made a huge statement for her race as well. The black woman with the can-do attitude paved the way for all the African-American talent that followed in her footsteps.

It's Not That Hard to Cheer Yourself On

Where do you start to change the way you speak to yourself? How do you find the positive words that will lift you up rather than put you down? You can start by making a list.

1. First write down your talents. What do you do well? A good shopper doesn't go to the store without a list, so start to feel good about yourself by putting your talents on paper.
2. What makes you happy? Make a list. This is vital because you won't be positive if you hate the things you do.

3. List your accomplishments. Everyone has accomplished things. They may seem ordinary to you, but they are a part of who you are. By writing them down, you will start to understand what others see as your best traits.

4. Take a look at your strengths and be proud of them. If you emphasize those strengths, the thoughts that hold you back will soon fade, as will many doubts and fears. Remember you can have the skills to do a job, but until you tell yourself you can do it, you will probably fail.

Praise Yourself!

If you are a parent, remember the time your child took his or her initial unsteady steps or said his or her first words. You praised them, bragged on them, hugged them, and made them feel like they were the most special person in the whole world. They were so thrilled by this praise that they tried to take another step or say even more words. Receiving praise was a vital part of their learning.

So when you accomplish something important in your life, even if it's small, you need to do the same thing for yourself. Tell yourself how proud you are of each positive thing you do.

I have known many people who have attempted to lose weight. Most of them would try every diet and start several different exercise programs. Many failed again and again because they went into the venture telling themselves they couldn't do it. Others who had positive attitudes going in but had their minds set only on the big goal failed as well. Their mind was so focused on the big picture that when they accomplished their first very important steps, they didn't stop and praise themselves for losing those first few pounds. Because the long-range goal seemed forever far away, their "self-talk" transformed into negative comments about how they were moving too slowly and they gave up.

No child goes from taking a step to winning gold in the Olympics in a week, and that holds true for adults as well. If Nola Ochs had not praised herself for each of her steps, she certainly never would have made it through her first community-college class, much less become a college graduate working on her master's degree.

The Yardstick Is Your Own

Many people are negative because they measure themselves against others. If you have never run, you are not going to go out your first day and match the times or distances of your neighbor who has jogged for years. Your initial goal needs to be jogging just a few steps one day and then equaling it the next. That is enough to allow yourself to praise your own efforts.

I don't like exercise. To me it seems like work, and I dread it. Yet I find when I simply go into a jog with a positive attitude, wearing a smile on my face, it becomes something I can enjoy. How do I accomplish that? I do it by thinking about my cousin who is suffering with MS and cannot even get out of her wheelchair. She would love to run, so when I consider what a blessing it is that I can run, I find I have more energy than I believed possible. When I change my attitude, the words I speak to myself are changed, and the jog becomes much easier.

Being able to do anything constructive is a joy we overlook, and we need to remind ourselves of that as we start each new task. If we think of each day of life as a blessing, the real joy of being positive begins to take over everything we do. And with that feeling in our hearts, the words that we speak to ourselves, as well as those we speak to others, will be positive as well.

A Proper Environment for a Positive Outlook

You have heard it all your life, but it's hard to stay positive about anything, including yourself, if you are surrounded by negative people and negative influences. If people are always putting you down, you are probably going to take some of those words to heart. Once you do your inventory and find things that are worth celebrating in your life, you don't need to be around those who revel in their own failures and unhappiness.

So step one in bringing a sense of value and self-worth to your self-communication is to push yourself away from friends who are negative or self-destructive. Some people just love to be miserable. They complain about everything and then blame everyone else for their problems.

They thrive in a world where they are surrounded by others with the same attitude. Even their thoughts are often filled with hate. They simply want to lash out and put others down to give themselves value. That is anything but a positive environment, and no one who wants to make a meaningful impact in the world needs to stay in that situation.

Negative Thoughts Show

People who carry around trash in their heads, people who have low self-esteem, people who are convinced they have little value, show that attitude in the way they look, walk, and talk.

I have a good friend who is just a normal-looking person. He would not be considered handsome, he is not an athlete, and he doesn't have many outstanding talents. Yet he is successful. Why? First, he understands what his strengths are and plays to them. Two, he looks in the mirror and likes who he sees. Three, he is always smiling. The wise man who discovered that happy people attract others discovered one of the keys to a successful life. And finally, no matter who is in a room, no matter their demographic group or social standing, Jim walks in believing he belongs with them. When he comes into a room, everyone seems to notice, and because he is sincerely glad to be there, they are glad to see him.

A Daily Cleanup

A friend once asked me, "Besides your family, who is the most important person in your life?"

I figured my friend was fishing for a compliment, so I said, "My best friend." But that wasn't the right answer.

I thought a bit more and rattled off, "My doctor? My pastor? My lawyer? My editor?" Each of my responses brought a smile and a shake of the head. Finally, after another dozen guesses, I gave up and asked, "Then who?"

"The garbage man," came the simple reply. "Ace Collins, you are the most positive person I know. Nothing keeps you down for long. A blue funk for you lasts just a few minutes. You always find ways to keep on the sunny side. But if the garbage man quit coming to your house, think how it would affect you. As the smell surrounded you, as the trash piled up all over your yard, as the flies and other pests swarmed into your home, you would become more and more unsettled. Things you once ignored would become huge problems. You would start to feel ill, you would lash out at your family and friends with harsh words, and your positive attitude would become harder and harder to maintain. Eventually you would fall under the weight of the trash and grow depressed. Therefore it is the garbage man who is the most important person in your life. He is the one who makes your world a positive one."

I thought about that analogy for a while and realized how inclusive it is. My friend was talking about the garbage on the outside of my world, but there is also the garbage that people carry around inside their head. Their homes may be spotless, but their minds are often filled with all the wrongs that have ever been done to them.

They constantly think about every grudge. They remember every mistake they have made. They continually plot ways to get even with enemies and are forever trying to come to grips with the times they have embarrassed themselves.

A human mind can carry around only so much garbage before that trash starts spewing out in our attitudes toward others and ourselves. The best way to keep a positive attitude is to get rid of your daily trash before you go to sleep each night. You can't help others until you clean out the trash inside yourself. It's not that hard to do either.

1. When you speak to yourself, admit your mistakes and realize that everyone makes them.

2. Work on ridding yourself of the baggage that you see in yourself.

3. Do things that make you happy. You can't change the past, but you can learn from it and move on. Don't let the past fester in your mind. Throw it away!

4. Catch yourself before you say something negative, and try to keep negative thoughts out of your head. Even if you have to make a sign and put it on your wall, embrace and remember the "I think I can" attitude.

5. Hold on to principles that you can be proud of and make them part of your dealings with others. I used to yell at officials at ballgames. Then I realized not only how stupid I looked but how it

affected me. I grew angry, I was unhappy, and I sure wasn't someone I would want to hang around with. When I saw that picture of myself, I realized I needed to change.

6. Seek hobbies that bring you joy and that you can share with others. I fix up old classic cars and drive them because I love the way that seeing these ancient vehicles makes others honk, wave, and smile. So find something that you like that brings positive emotions to others as well.

7. Realize that not everyone will like you or understand you. Will Rogers said he never met a man he didn't like. Will was a positive, upbeat man who considered each day of life such a sweet blessing that he probably did find something to like in everyone. But by the same token, a lot of folks were jealous of his happiness and success. So if someone wrongs you, pray for them, but don't lose sleep over the fact that they don't care for or understand you.

8. Like my friend Jim, look on the sunny side, and you will find a lot of people will be drawn to you. You will also discover that when you talk to yourself, even when you mess up, your words will be understanding, uplifting, and positive.

9. Finally, and probably most important, be yourself. Nola Ochs didn't worry about being out of place on a college campus, and because of her attitude,

she fit in just as well as the other students who were seventy years her junior. In the segregated era, Hattie McDaniel didn't run from her skin color but used it to elevate others by standing proudly at the top of her profession, thus paving the way for a new generation to be given better opportunities. Nola and Hattie liked themselves enough to thrive in worlds few like them would have dared enter. That is the key for each of us. If you are being who you are supposed to be, you will be happy.

Before we can use any of our words to lift anyone else up, we have to use them to elevate our own attitudes. We must have a can-do attitude before we can do anything for ourselves or others. So remember: the first person you need to impact with your words is yourself.

2

Write It Down

In 1816, Joseph Mohr was visiting his grandfather. On a cold winter's night, the young man made a long walk through the woods to the church. Mohr, who was a priest, found the beauty of that clear night and the deathly silence of the forest overwhelming. As he walked, the moon and stars lit his way and the only sound came from the snow crunching under his boots.

Mohr was so consumed by what he saw as the handiwork of God that he immersed himself in a solitary and silent prayer of thanksgiving. This feeling of natural awe was further fueled by the anticipation of his conducting a Christmas worship service. Never before had he felt so spiritually filled. Several hours later, still consumed by reverent wonder, Mohr sat down at a desk, determined to capture in prose what he had witnessed. When he finished, the young man reread his poem, made a few minor changes, and put it away.

Two years later, while serving as a priest in the town of Oberdorf, Austria, Mohr was presented with a much different holiday scene. On Christmas Eve, the organ at St. Nicholas Church gave up the ghost. The old instrument had long suffered various maladies, and this time all the priest's tinkering could not make it play even a single note. With his plans for a musical service now in chaos, a panicked Mohr raced through snow-packed streets to the home of his friend Franz Gruber.

Together the schoolteacher and the clergyman looked for a way to provide music for the holiday Mass. Gruber offered his skills as a guitarist, but then pointed out that none of the music that had been chosen would be appropriate for classical guitar. An anxious Gruber mused that they needed something new and fresh. They had to come up with something much different from anything they had ever used in a worship service, but what? With the clock ticking and the light of day giving way to the dark of night, Mohr remembered the poem he had written two years before. Racing back to his office, he pulled "Stille Nacht! Heilige Nacht!" from his desk. Gruber provided a tune, and the short bit of prose saved the St. Nicholas Christmas service of 1818.

Unlike most people, when he was struck by inspiration, Joseph Mohr wrote down his thoughts. If he had not expressed in verse what he observed and felt on a beautiful winter's night in 1816, two years later the clergyman could not have provided the song that saved the Christmas Eve worship service. And without the panic caused by the organ's dying, it's doubtful Mohr would have remembered that moonlit walk, much less recaptured the emotion needed to provide such a wonderful view of the first Christmas. The song was birthed only because the words had been penned when they were inspired, and not put off until it was more convenient.

Mohr had never intended for anyone else to read his poem. He wrote "Silent Night" only to capture his feelings in a private moment. Yet by penning his thoughts when his mind was filled with inspiration, the young priest had unknowingly produced a resource that not only would provide him with something he needed to save a special occasion, but also would grant millions a new look at a very special moment in time. "Silent Night" thus provides each of us with a model for recording the most important moments of life.

Why Write It Down Immediately?

Most of us don't write things down when events or experiences hit us emotionally. We might think of something and make a mental note of the importance of the idea or observation, but then most of us turn our attention to something else. And so our brilliant concepts often have the life span of a fruit fly. We are sure we will forever remember in detail a special moment in our lives, but in truth we rarely recall anything in detail.

Probably each of us has heard a wonderful joke that moved us to laughter, and vowed to share that bit of humor with someone else later in the day. Yet when the time comes, we've forgotten the elements that make the joke funny. Almost always a key line or phrase escapes us. When we try to retell the joke, it fails to have the same impact.

Gone with the Wind!

Everyone gets good ideas. Writers might think of a way to slant a chapter; speakers might find a new angle on a subject they have been asked to address; songwriters might come up with a new melody; or parents might think of specific advice for a child. Yet in our busyness, these great ideas, the ones we swear we will never forget, often get misplaced, and the idea that was going to change the world, or at least make a small impact on someone close to us, is lost forever.

Thoughts, inspiration, and observations that are recorded have a much better chance of being remembered. Thus, to make an impact with your words, you need to begin the habit of writing things down. Otherwise, your ideas will be gone with the wind.

Forgetting to Remember Means Forgetting

Lists are an essential part of our lives. We make them for all kinds of reasons. They are part of our history too. To ensure that Moses didn't forget ten very important commandments, he was told to write them down. To assure the citizens of the newly formed United States of America of their rights, the Bill of Rights was written down. Examples of historical lists go on and on, yet probably the most common lists are shopping lists. How many times have you realized you were out of something and made a mental note to put it on your shopping list later that day? Then the next time you needed that item, you realized that you had never placed it on the list. You forgot to remember, and so you forgot.

Or how many times have you gone to the store only to realize your list was still at home in the kitchen? As you walk the aisles and look at the shelves, you try to picture what was on the list. Yet even if you were the one who wrote the list, it's doubtful you can remember every item. Worse yet, going down every aisle at the store eats up a lot of time you could have used for something far more important, like spending time with your family. So on most occasions, forgetting the list makes the whole shopping trip a much more trying affair. Especially when you arrive home and find that the thing you needed most was the one thing you forgot.

It's a fact that making lists makes us more efficient. It keeps us organized. This is true at work, at home, and even while travelling. In reality a list is a very simple plan, an outline for a moment in your life.

A decade or so ago, I was at a family Christmas celebration. There were six grandchildren at the event. It seemed that because there were only six kids, no one felt the need to create a list. Well, after the presents were handed out, the need for a list became apparent.

Our youngest son had been forgotten. No one had bought him a present. Not only were his feelings hurt but the grandparents and a lot of uncles and aunts were more than a bit embarrassed.

At that same Christmas, an adult was forgotten too. The adults in the family had drawn names at Thanksgiving. It turned out that one of the adults hadn't written down the name of their person, got confused, and thought they had drawn the name of a different person, so one adult got two presents, while another got none.

Both situations could have been avoided if someone had just "written it down."

The History of Writing It Down

Though we don't know who was the first to write words on a clay tablet, we can probably be fairly certain about one thing: not long after, someone probably devised the first shopping list and promptly forgot it when they went to the market. Even at the very beginning, when the Mesopotamians were taking the world's first real stabs at a written language, someone forgot to buy the thing they needed most when they went shopping.

One of the first benefits of written language was that we no longer had to guess about history. Men and women wrote down much of their life stories. Thanks to the printed word, we have books and records that go back thousands of years, giving us insight into everything from laws to celebrations. When you look at some of the earliest surviving texts, it becomes obvious that it didn't take long for people to understand that writing helped to inspire and educate. It's hardly surprising that some of the most revered places in the world during the time of Moses were libraries. It was here that the wisdom of the ages was stored so that people wouldn't repeat the mistakes of previous generations.

Once writing became commonplace, almost everything of any importance was written down. Even in ancient Greece and Rome, minutes were kept during meetings. Births, deaths, and historic journeys were documented as well. And almost every speech a ruler or leader made was recorded. Yet the use of written words wasn't limited only to the ruling class or governments and historians. Once common people learned to write, the world really began to change.

On a Personal Level

Until the last few generations, recording daily thoughts and experiences in diaries and journals was a tradition. Everything from the important to the mundane was recorded, providing verbal snapshots of everyday life. The importance of such writings in helping us to understand our history and culture is unparalleled.

My grandfather was a poor Arkansas farmer. In a formal sense, he was not well educated, and he had little in the way of possessions. Yet beginning in his early years, he kept a journal. He recorded rainfall amounts, temperature changes, visits from friends and relatives, how much money he made from his crops and livestock, the death of friends and the birth of children, and even bits and pieces of the national and world news of the day. You can sense his fears as he wrote about those he knew who were off fighting in wars, and his joy in going fishing with a grandchild. Today, more than five decades after his death, those short entries in his journals provide me with a picture of the man, his life, and his personality. His words transport me to another place and time and give me such a good picture that I feel as if I am there. Though I barely knew my grandfather, my conception of the way he was and the way he lived, what he liked and how he thought, is clear indeed. Without those journals, I would hardly know him at all. Though he is gone, his words still live.

The Power of Journals

Two decades ago, I was with a good friend of mine in Houston. Louise was and remains a wise, compassionate person. On this trip, I told her the story of another friend from my college days who was battling cancer for the third time. Louise was so impressed with my verbal profile of Nancy that she wanted to meet her.

On a sunny afternoon, Louise, Nancy, and I met and talked for several hours. I could tell that Louise was deeply impressed with the sick woman's understanding of her situation and with the depth of her compassion for others who were battling the same disease. As we were leaving,

Louise told Nancy, "You need to keep a diary of everything you are going through. That way when someone else comes face to face with cancer, you can sharply remember what you were dealing with at the various stages of your battle and share those words with them."

Before she died, Nancy did just that, and her writings inspired another young cancer patient named Beth to keep fighting. Beth now has a husband, two kids, and an incredible life, at least in part because of the encouragement she received from reading Nancy's journal.

Nancy died at the age of thirty-three. At her funeral, I was overwhelmed by memories of this incredible young woman. At the service, I pulled out a pen and jotted down those memories on a piece of paper I found in the pew. Later that day, I asked others for insight into areas of Nancy's life I knew little about. Armed with what I had written down, I organized my scribbles into a story that I never really planned on publishing. I had penned it simply to remind myself about the incredible life Nancy had lived and to have something in future years I could turn to for inspiration.

A few months after I had written "Nancy's Story," I showed it to an editor at a local paper. Because he had known Nancy, I thought he would find it interesting on a personal level. I was shocked when he asked for permission to run it as an editorial. I had never thought about "Nancy's Story" striking a chord with those who didn't know her. The piece soon ran in a Waco, Texas, newspaper.

The story doesn't end there. An editor of a national magazine was given a copy of what had run in the newspaper. Ric Cox, an editor at *Plus Magazine*, asked me to expand the story, which I was able to do thanks to the notes I had made when the inspiration hit. Over time, Nancy's story, which is still on my website, has found its way into a book on women of faith, been read by millions, and been passed along to tens of thousands of cancer patients. None of these people would have been inspired by Nancy's story if Nancy and I had not followed Louise's suggestion to "write it down."

Beginning At Home: The Power of a Very Short Story

When you open a newspaper or magazine and see a dramatic photo, every nerve in your being takes note and hones in on the image. Not only are you touched but your curiosity is aroused. You want to know more. But what if there were no cutline below the photo or a feature story to go with the picture? You would be left to guess several things.

1. Who is it a picture of?
2. What happened?
3. When did it take place?
4. Where was it taken?
5. Why was it taken?

In magazine and newspaper stories, pictures don't stand alone. The who, what, where, when, and why are given beside or below the photo. In fact, if the story or cut-line wasn't provided, the editor of the publication would be inundated with letters and emails demanding the full story.

Now think of your own photos. If someone looked at them, would they have to guess at the who, what, when, where, and why?

I am always struck by sadness when I go to an antiques mall and see family photos and albums for sale. These photos, some more than a hundred years old, were taken for a reason, but because there is no writing on the back of the images, they now have no real value. These striking pictures no longer tell the stories they were meant to tell. One of the greatest services we can pay to our family and friends is to write down the stories of our most precious photos. At the very least, each picture should be labelled with names and dates and, if possible, the where and why too.

Like my grandfather's journals, photos bring events and people into sharper focus. They are priceless records of a moment in history. Yet those moments are often lost when the person who took the pictures doesn't pen the rest of the story on the back of them. Such words bring these images to life. If you write it down, then your photos will have a better chance of playing an important part in your family for generations to come instead of ending up in the antiques mall or the trash bin.

Writing Preserves the Present for the Future

Letters were once people's main means of communication. And they were rarely short. People often wrote page after page of news. When you read old letters, you find a lot of wonderful and inspirational stories. Letters written during wars are classic examples. The world is much richer for knowing what Abraham Lincoln, Winston Churchill, and other great leaders went through during their most trying days. Yet an even greater understanding of personal sacrifice comes in knowing what the not-so-famous were thinking and doing during those times.

I had an uncle who was stationed in the Aleutian Islands during World War II. There were many times during the battles that he could actually see the faces of the Japanese men he was fighting. After one especially fierce skirmish, the American forces overran the enemy camp and found that all of the Japanese soldiers had fought to their deaths. There would be no captives to interrogate that day, so it would seem that the stories of who these men really were would be forever lost.

As the men searched the enemy camp, my uncle Troy picked up a small notebook. Since the words were in Japanese, my uncle had no idea what was written in the notebook, but he carried it with him through the remainder of the war. It went across the Pacific, landed on several islands, and finally found its way into the jungles of Burma.

After VJ day, Uncle Troy and that notebook came home to Arkansas.

For many years, my uncle stored the notebook in a trunk with other mementos from his time as a soldier. One day, while looking for something in his old footlocker, he came across the decades-old pages covered with writing he still could not comprehend. Feeling the need to understand the mind of a man he had once fought, he did a little research and located a Japanese consulate. With two purposes in mind, he arranged to take the notebook to the agency. He wanted to have the words translated so he could know what the writer was thinking as he struggled in the horrific conditions on the Aleutian Islands, and he wanted to see that the notebook was placed in the hands of the man's family.

When translated, the notebook revealed a man whose emotions during the war mirrored my uncle's. The Japanese soldier was homesick. He deeply missed his wife and children. His words spoke of all the birthdays and family milestones he had missed and the war that in many ways made no sense to him. He hated killing and at times he thought the fighting would drive him mad. Yet as he shared his most personal thoughts, as well as his doubts and fears, what came through time and again was how proud he was to have his family's love. It was that love and his hope to experience it again in person that enabled him to get through each day. Reading that journal allowed my uncle to finally bury any animosity he had for the Japanese people and to make peace with an old foe. In a very real sense, the war had finally come to an end for him.

It took a lot of work and several years, but Uncle Troy made sure the man's family received the journal, and he established a bond with the children of his onetime enemy. That soldier's thoughts and even his life came to have so much more meaning simply because he took a few moments each day to "write it down."

The Loss of the Written Word

Letter writing and journal keeping began to die as a common practice as the use of the telephone grew. Thanks to the immediacy of the phone, personal stories again became largely oral presentations. That was great for the moment, but in the long term, many wonderful tales and experiences that might have been shared with others who could have read them years later were lost forever.

Other substitutes for the written word emerged as film and video began to crowd out written histories. At first, recording the important moments of life in a visual format seemed wonderful. But as technology changes, the means of viewing old film and video are being lost. Very few people have Super-8 movie projectors anymore, and now VCRs are disappearing from people's homes. Many are predicting that standard DVD players will be obsolete in less than a decade, replaced by something new. Unfortunately, only a small percentage of home movies and videos have been converted to forms compatible with new devices.

Because they don't require playback devices, memories written in letters, scrapbooks, or journals will outlast those recorded in other media, just as easy to share now as they were a century ago. So if you're interested in keeping your most important and cherished moments alive, you have to write them down.

Making an Impact

For your words to make a lasting impression, someone has to record them. Otherwise, they are lost forever, as are the important things you have witnessed in your life, things that could inspire and positively impact people for generations to come.

Though Joseph Mohr's writing down his feelings immediately after his memorable walk through the woods was responsible years later for saving the Christmas Eve service at St. Nicholas Church in 1818, we wouldn't be singing the carol today if another man hadn't written his song down.

We don't know the identity of the individual who came by the small Austrian church to fix the broken organ in the days following the Christmas Eve service. What we do know is that the repairman asked the priest what the church did for music at the Christmas Mass without an organ. Mohr not only explained the story of that December 24th service but played and sang his song for the man. The repairman was so impressed that he wrote the words and music down on paper. Over the next thirty years, the repairman left copies of "Silent Night" in every city where he stopped to fix an organ or a piano. As a result, "Silent Night" has been sung by more people than any other song in history.

If you see or think of something worth remembering, take a moment to record it. Don't put it off until it's too late; do it immediately. Then, like Joseph Mohr, you will have those words ready when you need to share them with others.

3

Saying Thanks

In September of 1814, the United States was at war with England. William Beane of Upper Marboro, Maryland, was one of the few men in the area not directly involved in the fighting. Yet just because he didn't wear a uniform didn't mean the elderly Beane wasn't serving his country. He was a doctor by trade, but he had also been entrusted with the position of city magistrate.

Late one night, Beane's sleep was interrupted by the catcalls of two drunken British troopers. Picking up his gun and badge, Beane rounded up the soldiers and deposited them in the town's jail, setting into motion a series of events that became an important part of American history and tradition.

When the two redcoats did not return to their camp, the English commander sent out a search party. Told his men had been arrested, the officer became so incensed that he had the doctor arrested and placed on a prison ship in Baltimore Harbor.

When they discovered Beane had been incarcerated, the citizens of Upper Marboro banded together to gain their beloved physician's freedom. Pooling their resources, they sought the skills of a well-known Maryland attorney, Francis Scott Key. After studying the case and making the necessary requests, Key gained a meeting with British Admiral Alexander Cochrane. In the informal court proceeding that took place on the evening of September 3, Key argued that Beane had simply been doing his job and that it was the two English troopers who were the guilty parties. Cochrane remained unmoved by the attorney's contentions and ruled that for his crimes Beane would be confined until the war's end. Before the doctor could be taken from the admiral's quarters, Key retrieved a stack of letters from his coat pocket. After making a show of untying the string by which they were bound, the lawyer handed the letters to Cochrane.

"Before you condemn Dr. Beane," Key said, "you need to read these letters."

Cochrane ordered the guards not to remove the prisoner, then, taking a seat behind his desk, began to review the letters. For five minutes nothing was said, the only sound being the rustling of paper as Cochrane studied each of the pages. Finally the officer looked back at Key and Beane, took a deep breath, and said, "As soon as the upcoming battle is concluded, you can return home. What I have read proves the outstanding character of Dr. Beane."

Eleven days later, on September 14, Beane and Key were still in British custody. After two weeks of preparation, the battle for Fort McHenry now raged at a fever pitch. At sunrise, when the cannon fire stopped and the smoke cleared, Key borrowed a telescope and aimed it at the Americans' position. The attorney felt great relief as he spied the Stars and Stripes still defiantly flying over the battered fort. At first the vision of that flag moved the lawyer to tears; then it inspired him to take a pencil and paper and compose a poem he titled "The Defense of Fort McHenry." Later, those words were published in newspapers throughout the United States, and when set to music, they became "The Star Spangled Banner."

What had proven Beane's character? What had been written in the letters Key produced that had so deeply affected the British admiral's verdict? What was the reason Key had been retained and then detained? What set in motion the events that led to the writing of America's national anthem? Words not only freed Beane, but the fear of what Beane and Key might tell the Americans had placed the lawyer in the right place to pen words that would inspire his native country for generations.

The notes that freed Dr. Beane were written by British soldiers who were badly injured during the war. Although the soldiers were enemies of his country, Beane had used his skills to save their lives. Many of those who had felt the compassionate hand of the good doctor had taken the time to write to him declaring their thanks for his actions. Without those thank-you notes, who knows what would have become of Dr. William Beane or what Americans would now be singing as their national anthem?

A History of the Thank-You Note

Thank-you letters or notes can be traced back thousands of years. While most of the early thank-you letters have been lost, a few are still known and cherished by people all around the globe. When the apostle Paul thanked the young churches in his letters, his written words became an essential element of the New Testament. Paul's thank-you letters, meant for only a few men and women, have had an extraordinary impact on hundreds of millions on every corner of the globe, demonstrating how powerful and long lasting a thank-you note can be.

Paul didn't start the habit of acknowledging gifts with kindness, nor did the habit end with him. In the Dark Ages, when a lord sent a neighboring lord gifts through a courier, the courier returned with a note of thanks to acknowledge that the courier had delivered the goods. This probably began the common use of a thank-you letter for a specific favor or gift.

With the advent of inexpensive postal service in the 1800s, millions from all classes began thanking others for acts of kindness with mailed notes and letters. These notes can be found in libraries, family Bibles, and attic trunks. In fact, for generations the need to acknowledge a gift or favor was the primary reason for a majority of personal letters.

The Custom Falls out of Favor

Until the past twenty years, thank-you notes and letters were not just a commonly employed form of correspondence but were an expected response for gifts, acts of kindness, and services. As a result, parents taught their children the importance of writing thank-you notes, and writing thank-you notes was part of the curriculum at most schools. Yet thanks to cheap long-distance telephone service, thank-you notes began to fall out of favor in the last part of the twentieth century. A call was quicker and easier than penning a note, so many people began to dial in their thanks.

Today, the custom of writing formal thank-yous has nearly dropped out of existence. Recent surveys indicate that a very low percentage of thank-you notes are sent out even for wedding, baby, and graduation gifts, and rarely does anyone ever mail a thank-you for birthday gifts. Once it was common to write thank-yous to doctors, repairmen, teachers, or mechanics. Today hardly anyone feels the need to do so.

The trend of not writing thank-you notes is made even sadder because the tools of the information age have actually made saying thanks easier than ever before. It's a snap to buy stamps; thank-you cards and stationery are inexpensive; and addresses can be found simply by logging on to the web. Though picking up a pen and writing a message of thanks seems to be an act few feel compelled to tackle, if we want to make the words we use each day count, we need to reclaim this honored tradition.

When to Write a Thank-You

Even in a modern age, a considerate person needs to always acknowledge any kind act or gift with a thank-you.

Saying thanks, no matter how you do it, has real power! Not saying thanks seems to say not only that you did not appreciate a gift or an act of kindness but also that you don't value the giver.

The most powerful thank-you is still sent via mail.

My literary agent recently gave me a penholder for my desk. My thank-you mentioned the gift and then added that in the future I would sign all of my contracts with a pen taken from that holder. I concluded by saying that keeping the penholder on my desk would remind me daily just how important his efforts are to my work.

A note like this takes very little time, but it means a great deal. Not only do you assure the giver that the gift is appreciated but, more important, you assure them that you appreciate what they have brought to your life.

Advice for Writing Thank-You Notes

When writing a thank-you, a handwritten note or letter is best. An important rule to follow is that even if you purchase a card that has a wonderful printed message, you should add a few lines to personalize your response.

When thanking someone for an act or a gift, your note needs to include personal information. Mention the gift or action that has prompted your writing, express how much it is appreciated and how you will use it, and finally offer some tie to symbolize the relationship between you and the giver. As an example, if the gift was a book, then you can cite a passage that moved you and mention how thinking of those words will always remind you of them. If you were given an umbrella, you might share that the gift reminds you that even in the storms of life, they have always been there for you. The key is making sure that they understand not only that you appreciate the gift but also how much they mean to you.

If you have bad penmanship or are composing a lengthy letter, using a computer to compose and then print out your thank-you is acceptable. But if you go this route, it's even more important that you make sure your words have impact. Don't just fire off a note that reads like a generic thank-you; create copy that proves you value the time, effort, and expense it took to pick out and send the gift or to accomplish the service. You simply can't live without friends; you need them in every period of your life. Yet relationships are often much more fragile than people realize. A simple thank-you just might create a bond that will bring support for years to come.

Email

No one can argue that email has a huge advantage in speed over standard postal replies. A thank-you via email is direct and immediate, but its impact is limited because it's so easy to do. Email is best employed for spontaneous thank-yous that acknowledge an act of kindness, an unexpected inspiration, or a meaningful action.

A few examples of using email in this way would be to thank someone for emailing you a greeting (birthday, anniversary, etc.) or an inspiring message. An email message is also a wonderful way to quickly note a special deed that you witnessed. Why note a good deed? Simply because it might become a platform that encourages others to continue to lift others up. A thank-you of any kind can inspire people into action, even the simple action of continuing to give an extra smile or a kind word in their fields of service. Maybe you saw a friend stop to help a stranded motorist or reach out to an elderly person or a child in need of assistance. Their act might seem insignificant to them until you show them how much it inspired you. It's also a great way to point out something wise you heard someone say in a conversation or a speech.

A Call or a Text Message

Cell phones have dramatically changed our lives. We are now rarely out of touch. If someone helped you at a meeting or with a small problem, a text message or a call can be used to say thanks. But texting or calling should not be used instead of written thank-yous for more valued gifts or services.

Making a Big Impact with a Simple Thank-You

More than twenty years ago, not long after my first book hit the market, I remembered the influence a high-school teacher had on my life. In her class, I started to believe I had the talent to use words. For days I felt this urge to get in contact with Miss Jones, but I didn't know where to start. Finally, I phoned my old high school.

I talked to several people there until I found one who remembered my English teacher. I was told she had left the school and moved to one on the other side of the state. So I called the school she had moved to. They did not remember her, but the principal gave me the name of a retired administrator who might. When I contacted him, he recalled Miss Jones had left their school to teach in a small town in Wisconsin. I then called the school in that state and discovered Miss Jones had retired and was living in a neighboring community. Information gave me her number. I called, reintroduced myself, told her what I was doing, then jotted down her address. As soon as the call concluded, I wrote a thank-you note that I mailed with a signed copy of one of my books.

In this case, all I was trying to do was show Miss Jones how much she had meant to me, but I found out later that this simple act had meant the world to her. One thank-you somehow convinced this outstanding educator that her thirty years of teaching had stood for something special. I know of several others whose lives had been deeply influenced by Miss Jones; can you imagine how she would have felt if all of them had written to her as well?

Who Has Impacted You?

No matter what your age, there is a coach, pastor, doctor, neighbor, old boss, coworker, Sunday school teacher, or former neighbor who has dramatically affected your life. In truth, as you look back over your history, you will probably note that more than one person has impacted you. Now the question you must answer is, "Do they know what they did for me?"

There are countless people in our lives we need to thank, but never have. We need to take a few moments each year to do a new inventory of these folks. If you have never considered this element of your life, then begin by reviewing your early childhood. Consider the people whose positive input changed you in a special way. Their words or actions may have been responsible for the direction you chose or the successes you have had.

If your mind is a bit fuzzy on who impacted you at various stages of your development, do some research. Pull out old family albums or school yearbooks. As you study those old photographs, memories will come alive, and you will recall the influence of old friends, mentors, and special family members. As those memories come to life, pick up a pen and paper and jot down the names of those who impacted you in the past.

Once you have covered your childhood, start thinking about those who influenced you in your adult life. If you are a parent, there are people who helped with your kids who need to be thanked. Probably there are also former neighbors, coworkers, employees, or church members who were there for you during difficult times. You will soon discover that when you jot down the names of all those who have impacted or blessed your life, the list is long, but what a precious list it is. Your life simply would not be what it is without each of these men and women. Do they know how you feel? Have you used your words to show them the impact they have made in your life? If not, now is the time!

Thanking the Inspirations in Your Life

Some of the folks you need to thank will be easy to find. They may still live close to you or may have kept in contact with you over the years. As you go through your list, note those you can easily find and begin by writing to them.

As you compose your notes, remember that those receiving them will be surprised. They won't be expecting you to express your gratitude for something they did for you so long ago. So before you write, imagine what it will mean to them to know that they so influenced and blessed you. As you write, be direct and honest, and allow your emotions to be evident in your words. Make sure you define what the person did for you and how much they mean to you. Let them know you feel blessed for having had them in your life and that you thank God for their influence. Most important, don't worry about literary rules, style, or tone. Allow your heart to be heard, and let your words flow with emotion.

If the person you feel a need to thank has died, send the thank-you note and the reasons for it to one of their relatives. A spouse, son, daughter, brother, sister, or other relative will be deeply touched by your thoughts.

Your words will bring comfort, joy, tears, and inspiration. It will remind them of the wonderful things their loved one did while they walked on the earth.

If you don't know where someone lives now, don't write them off as hopelessly lost. The tools for finding anyone are right at your fingertips. With the internet you can usually uncover almost anyone's street address, phone number, or email address in less than fifteen minutes. So use the search engines, and if that fails, then use these same search engines to find one of the person's family members or friends. Surely one of them can help you locate the person who needs to hear your words of thanks.

Making a Weekly Impact

Probably you won't be able to tackle your whole list in a single sitting. Writing just one note can be draining. After all, you aren't thanking someone for a small gift; you're thanking them for impacting your life in a special way. Find a calendar and mark a day each week when you will have the time to write a letter of special thanks to someone who has influenced your life.

But don't stop there. Continue to find people to thank. Continue to look back and be reminded of others who impacted you in some way and add them to your list. Maybe a story in the paper or on the TV and radio news has inspired you to do something. When that happens, write the reporter or the news anchor and share how their work moved you. Look around you when you shop, note people who are going the extra mile, then acknowledge them by writing a short note. If a church, school, or business is doing something great, write them. You can find inspiration and heroes all around you. Your words might well be the driving force that keeps them going. So find a new person or group to thank each week and send them a note or letter!

Heroes Around Us

Five years ago, I watched a lovely young cheerleader perform at a Baylor University basketball game. Her smile lit up the whole arena. Though she was less than five feet tall and missing her left hand, Kaytlin Do was a giant when it came to integrity, compassion, and courage.

Even without her left hand, Kaytlin performed the same difficult stunts as the other cheerleaders. In fact, she did it so well, few in the crowd realized she was technically handicapped. This young woman immediately became one of my heroes.

As season-ticket holders, my family had the chance to get to know Kaytlin. As we visited with her, we discovered she was even more beautiful on the inside than on the outside. Her inner strength and faith gave her the courage not just to try anything but to do anything. It seemed that nothing could hold her back. Remarkably, her story hardly seemed likely to produce this kind of achievement.

Kaytlin's parents escaped Vietnam before she was born. Growing up as an Asian in North Texas made her stand out. That would be hard on any teenager, but couple that with the fact she was missing her left hand and she had every reason to retreat into a tight shell. Yet what might have caused others to give up drove Kaytlin to excel.

What I didn't know was that even as she gained an academic scholarship to a major university and became captain of her college cheerleading squad, there were times she lacked a certain degree of self-confidence.

After two years of marveling at her attitude and talents, I wrote Kaytlin a letter. In my note I shared the reasons she had inspired my family. As I composed my words, I had no idea that my thanking this college kid for so impacting my family's lives would have much impact on her. It would be months before I discovered my letter had come at just the right time — a moment when she had been feeling down.

A few weeks later, after a game, a little girl, born with only one hand, came up and hugged Kaytlin. The child's parents later told Kaytlin that their little girl had been teased in class ever since preschool, causing her to become withdrawn. She was eight when she first noticed Kaytlin. Watching the smiling college girl fly through the air and lead thousands in cheers inspired her to try a few things herself. She began with gymnastics and then moved on to other sports. Even though she lacked a hand, she found she had the heart and the will to accomplish almost anything. With this new success, her shyness disappeared. She too wrote Kaytlin, thanking her for being her inspiration.

A few weeks after the small girl's letter arrived, Kaytlin shared this story with me. I was shocked when I discovered that Kaytlin, who had accomplished so much, had for years harbored great anger in being born so different from everyone else. But when she discovered she had inspired that little girl, the rage melted away.

Kaytlin is out of college now and has achieved great success in the business world. Yet even as the awards and honors have poured in, she has not forgotten the impact of a couple of thank-yous on her life. Those thank-you notes proved to this young woman that she did indeed have something to share with the world and that she could be a hero—a bright shining light of inspiration for others. When she is not on the job, you will likely find Kaytlin at the burn ward of a Dallas–Fort Worth children's hospital. She is there to show children firsthand how anyone can exceed expectations and overcome handicaps.

Would Kaytlin have worked with disabled kids if it had not been for a couple of thank-you notes? I don't know. But I do know that even heroes are inspired when they are told they are making a difference. I also know that heroes are all around each of us. Look for them. They might be older folks who served in a war, teachers who go the extra mile, volunteers at a hospital, or people who live just down the street. Everyone needs to be told they are special. It fuels their fire and keeps them going. So in truth, you will never run out of people to thank, even if you set a goal of thanking a new person every week.

Changing the World

As children we may have grumbled when we were forced to write thank-you notes. But through this discipline, our parents taught us that thank-yous can be one of the most powerful ways you can use words. A thank-you speaks volumes about your character, humbleness, and values. It points out that you realize that those who reach out to others mean a great deal to you. Your thank-you will inspire them to continue to reach out. Your actions will also put into focus the value of all those who have touched and who will continue to touch your life. Your thank-yous will also remind them of the value of their actions.

In the case of Dr. Beane, his kindness and the thank-you letters he received didn't just buy his freedom; they led to Francis Scott Key's writing "The Star Spangled Banner." Paul's letters of thanks have impacted people's faith for two thousand years. Think of the kids Kaytlin is inspiring! Who knows what kind of power your sincere words will have. They might well renew an old bond, inspire someone who is down, change the direction of a life, or remind a person that their life has really mattered.

I have found that writing and saying thanks will also set the person you thanked on a quest to thank others. Presented in a sincere way, shared for the obvious and the not-so-obvious reasons, thank-yous can and do have an incredible influence.

4

Greetings

My youngest son, Rance, left for college two years ago. After looking at several different state and private universities, he found himself attending a small, private school in Arkansas. During one of his first calls home, he voiced an observation about student behavior that might surprise you. It seemed that everywhere he went, people looked him in the eye, smiled, and said hi. He couldn't go anywhere without having students, teachers, and employees waving and belting out a strong, friendly greeting. Yet this was just the beginning of the culture shock he experienced.

He told me, "Dad, you can't walk anywhere alone either. If you're walking across campus, soon someone is walking along with you. Even if they don't know you, they strike up a conversation. And in the cafeteria, if you're sitting alone, someone always asks if they can join you."

How much better would you feel if everywhere you went people smiled and said a sincere hello? How much better would our world be if everybody followed this practice?

Saying Hello Opens Up a
Bright World of Opportunity

In the last forty years, Wal-Mart has moved from being a small Arkansas retailer to a worldwide institution. Their growth is unparalleled. Yet with all the company's new product lines, larger and larger superstores, and expansion to seemingly every corner of the globe, Wal-Mart still employs the simple practice of saying hello. When you go into a Wal-Mart, someone is always there to greet you at the door.

Wal-Mart has greeters for a reason. Sam Walton, the company's founder, was a real people person. In his hometown of Bentonville, Arkansas, he would say hello to everyone as he walked down the town's streets. He was always waving at friends from his pickup truck too. He required that this practice be carried out in his stores, because he realized that when a customer is greeted, that customer no longer feels as if he or she is just one of the masses. Because of that greeting, that customer has become an individual. This practice has worked so well for Wal-Mart it has been picked up by scores of other retailers. So why hasn't it been picked up by more people on the street? Why aren't we friendlier?

Are You Crazy?

As I thought about what Rance was experiencing at Ouachita Baptist University, I decided to try a little experiment. Whenever I was walking down a street or out shopping at a mall or store, I thought about smiling. When someone looked my way, I nodded and offered in an enthusiastic but moderate tone, "Hello. How are you?" Many people raced on by without saying anything, but a few responded and smiled back. Some, whom I had met before, even stopped and struck up a conversation.

When I proposed to a few of my friends and family that they try "this greeting thing," they shook their heads and said, "People will think I'm crazy."

I had to agree. I had gotten a few strange looks from people as I greeted them. But at least my smile and friendly hello got them to think. If they concluded I was a few bricks shy of a load, that didn't matter to me, because in spite of all those who thought I was crazy, I discovered more than a handful of other folks who really enjoyed having someone say hello to them.

There were other benefits as well. As I practiced greeting people regularly, I found I had more energy in my step and a much more positive attitude about every facet of my life. What caused it? I think mostly it was just my smiling. I have found that even smiling while I am in a car makes me feel a lot better about traffic jams. It's all about attitude, and if you are happy in your own world, those around you will want you to share a bit of that happiness with them. So if for no other reason than feeling good, develop the "smile and greet habit."

But I Can't Do That ...

One of the most common excuses I have heard for not giving others an enthusiastic greeting is that the person is too shy. This excuse has also kept millions from experiencing some of the best moments in life. Being shy is no excuse. Even shy people can smile and say hello. And just the act of doing so slowly brushes away a bit of the shyness and opens the door for meaningful contact.

Being too busy is probably the number-one excuse for not being friendly. If your mind is crowded with a wide variety of problems, if you are constantly looking at the clock and worrying that you will miss an appointment, then you might well think you are too busy. But no one is too busy to look up and say hello to others.

I once heard football coach Lou Holtz say, "You should take your work seriously and you should take your spouse seriously, but you should never take yourself seriously." If the too-busy people of the world adopted this philosophy, they would begin to smile more, start looking around and seeing the beauty of the world, and actually start saying hello to those around them. And they would still get just as much work done.

A Smile and a Hello Work Wonders

For years I have watched simple smiles open up hearts. A few years ago, I had season tickets for Baylor University basketball games. One of the cheerleaders, Bailey, possessed a smile that lit up the whole arena. It made me feel good every time I saw her smile. The usher for our section had that same great smile and always greeted everyone who came into her section. Even on nights I was dead tired and had fought rainstorms and traffic to get to the game, these two women made me feel good. And before the year was over, I personally thanked them for it. Today, when I think of either person, I still feel a warm surge of happiness rush through my heart. These women are still positively affecting my attitude several years later through their greetings to me.

There is a woman in our church whose smile and sincere greeting do the same thing. I simply can't feel down when I am around Julie. Every time I see her, I feel better than I did before hearing her hello. Julie is a nurse at a hospital, and I have to believe that her positive attitude and warm greetings have done as much good as all the medicine in the building.

If all of us had the attitude of these three women, the days would be a lot sunnier not just for those around us but for ourselves as well. After all, a smile and a kind word are things you not only receive but also pass on.

Greetings Can Change the World

Back in the late 1950s and early 1960s, America was still very much a divided nation. In the South, racial lines were still clearly drawn. Schools, churches, and even entertainment venues had separate sections for blacks and whites. The lines between those sections were not to be crossed.

My grandparents lived in Salem, Arkansas, which was an all-white community in the Ozark foothills. One day in the early 1960s, Grandpa was strolling across the town square on his lunch break from his job at the post office. As he walked by the bus depot, a friendly voice called out to him.

"Tom ... Tom Shell, is that you?"

Glancing to his left, Grandpa found himself looking into the face of a man he hadn't seen for almost fifty years. He and Ben had lived down the road from each other as children. They often played together as their parents worked the neighboring family farms. Grandpa had even occasionally gone to church with Ben and his family. Yet when it came time to attend school, the boys' days together ended. Grandpa enrolled at the white school and Ben at the one for African-Americans. At that moment the racial divide that had not been important during the first six years of their lives was suddenly and silently accepted by both as law.

Over time, both of the families moved from their Izard County farms. Grandpa and Ben grew up and lost track of each other. Their lives remained as separate as the signs marked "white" and "colored." Because they were prevented from bumping into each other in spots like theaters or restaurants, the two might never have seen each other again if Ben had not had to make a bus connection in Salem that day.

Grandpa was overjoyed to see this smiling face from his past. The two sat down on the square and filled each other in on all the details of their lives. Noting the time, Grandpa asked Ben if he would join him for lunch. It was then the racial divide again reared its ugly head. Ben explained to Grandpa that a black man could not eat at the local cafe.

Up until that moment, my grandfather had essentially been a closet racist. He had gone along with the status quo never considering the pain it created. Now, when forced to face that image, he did not like what he saw. Suddenly he realized it was time for a "makeover." Rather than accept the great divide, he decided to do something about it. He took Ben to the cafe, where they sat at a table, and together the two of them broke the color line.

My grandfather would continue to visit with Ben for many years. They even went to some family reunions together. The color of the skin no longer mattered; instead, there was only the bond of a friendship forged in childhood play and then reborn with a smile and a friendly greeting. Consider what both men would have missed if Ben had been too shy to speak.

The Places You Feel Welcome

For more than twenty years, I have made a weekly trip to a nonprofit organization in Dallas commonly known as WME (World Missionary Evangelism), which runs children's homes, provides food and medical centers, builds schools, and drills wells in many third-world countries. The people who work at this organization are incredibly busy. To make sure that a large percentage of donors' gifts are used to fund overseas projects, WME operates with what many would call a skeleton staff. It seems that everyone at the office does two or three jobs. Yet whenever I arrive at their headquarters, each member of the staff always takes a moment to smile and welcome me. They make me feel as if I'm a special guest.

The WME staff's warm greetings do not end with my visits. I have also observed that UPS and FedEx delivery people, as well as every other person who walks through the door, are made to feel special. I'm guessing that the way they greet visitors has a great deal to do with their success in their projects around the world. People can sense sincerity, and putting people first always makes an impact.

Think for a moment about the places where you feel the most welcome and then consider why you feel so good about being there. The top reason is probably because someone there greets you warmly and makes you feel like they are thrilled to see you.

Now ask yourself: Do you respond in the same way when someone comes into your world? Are you making your home, your place of business, or even the neighborhood where you live a place where others feel welcome? The formula for doing this is easy, but many fail to follow it:

1. Smile. The first thing we all should do when meeting another person is smile. It doesn't make any difference whether this is the first time you have met them or the thousandth, a smile breaks down barriers and assures the other person you are

happy to see them. They will be ready to listen to you if you start every meeting with a smile.

2. Body Language. As important as your smile, your posture when greeting someone speaks volumes. If you are slumping around or holding back, your welcome is muted at best. If you are relaxed and leaning toward the person, your verbal greeting carries much more weight.

3. Enthusiasm. If you want someone to feel welcome, be enthusiastic about seeing them. The tone of your voice will be a good indication of how much you care about their entering your world. A mumbled greeting indicates you would just as soon not see them. So combine your smile and your body language into a human exclamation point that assures everyone you are happy they are there.

4. Warmth. When you think about the people you look forward to seeing, a sense of warmth almost always floods your heart. Many people hold back warmth, almost as if saving it for a special day. But if you put it away like fine china that never gets used, no one will feel welcome to come into your world. I have been in many businesses and even churches that lack warmth. Good things are happening behind the walls, but no one seems to want to share them. In time, places that lack warmth shrivel like a cut flower. So do people.

5. Sincerity. If you sincerely care about someone, it comes across. Sincerity requires you to open your heart and allow your emotions to really shine through. Sadly, many people are as afraid to do this as they are to smile for a photograph.

It's a Wonderful Life, So Show It

Many of us wallow in our problems and fail to realize that they are really overshadowed by our blessings. That's why so many people walk down the street with their heads and eyes down, never greeting anyone with a smile or a hello. They are going through life thinking everything they do is a wasted effort.

If you have ever watched the classic Frank Capra film *It's a Wonderful Life*, then you know how most of us see the world. Jimmy Stewart's character, George Bailey, is downcast and depressed, convinced he has failed in everything he has ever done. Meanwhile, the film's villain, Henry Potter, always seems to be smiling and reveling in the pain he causes others. Then comes George's revelation. He finds that he is the one who has the treasure that matters. He is the one with the great friends and wonderful family.

When George figures things out, he races through the streets seeing all the beauty that he had previously ignored. He greets friends in a manner that is part craziness and all sincerity. It's obvious he is thrilled to be alive and ecstatic to be joyfully living each moment of his life. All it took for this to happen was a new perspective. The choice to change his attitude was his own. As the movie shows us, before he became depressed, George had smiled and gone out of his way to be wonderful to others all of his life. So was it any wonder that those whom he had touched embraced him during his time of greatest need? Meanwhile, Potter, who never had a kind word for anyone, ended up having great wealth but no one to share it with. His happiness was a sham.

If you start each day thinking of George Bailey and his greetings to those he met on the street, and how his words and attitude impacted an entire town, you will brighten a great many people's days. Remember, with the right attitude, it is a wonderful life, and that life needs to be shared.

Changing the Mood

So much of life today is confrontational. As a school principal, my wife constantly found herself resolving conflict. She discovered that much anger could be defused by the way she greeted each situation.

One student from a rough home seemed constantly to be at odds with a history teacher. Many times this resulted in a shouting match and Brad's being escorted to my wife's office. Kathy always greeted Brad with a smile, which calmed him down, then sought to find out what caused his outburst. Finally, she handed out a fair punishment.

As the school year continued, whenever she saw Brad, she greeted him with a big smile and an enthusiastic

"How are you?" He simply couldn't help but return that greeting with a grin. In time Brad began to value my wife's friendship so much he changed his combative nature and stayed out of trouble. Kathy made such a deep impression with her positive greetings that Brad often stopped by her office just to check in and visit. Imagine a high school principal's office becoming a warm place to drop in!

I have seen Kathy use this positive, friendly method to defuse a great many potentially explosive confrontations with students, teachers, and parents. Most of the time, she was able not only to deal satisfactorily with an issue but also to gain a great deal of respect in the process. And it all began with the way she greeted the person coming to see her.

I have seen this approach work in all areas of life. Even referees, often the most hated individuals in sports, can better control the game, the players, and the crowd if they begin with a smile and a kind word before the game.

Beyond the Street

For my job, I have to spend a lot of time on the telephone. When I'm not interviewing people, I am being interviewed. I've learned that a smile and genuine happiness can be heard through a phone. I also know that a short call can mean a great deal to people.

Every August 17th, I can count on Buford Ward to call me and wish me a happy birthday. I went to church with Buford for several years, and even now he still remembers to call. Our conversation is never long, yet the sincere words we share prove the bond is still there. Naturally, when I see him on the street or in a store, I can't wait to visit with him. I am guessing that Buford calls a lot of folks on their birthdays, and I'm sure all of them treasure that call as much as I do.

When someone calls you, allow your voice and your words to say, "It's great to hear from you!" Imagine what that will mean to the person on the other end of the line. When you make the call, make that other person feel important as well. Your greeting will help kick-start your conversation in a direction that will probably lift the spirits of both of you during the call and long after.

You Can Always Find a Good Reason

A phone greeting can have the same impact as saying hello on the street. And making a call is about the easiest thing any of us can do.

A birthday call means a great deal to people; it always brings a smile. Best of all, with a simple calendar or a computer program to remind you of each important date, it's easy to keep up with birthdays and anniversaries. So don't just stop with the card; back it up with a call.

On days when you don't have birthdays, call a friend or a family member to check in with them. It can make a huge impact. One of the best ways to fully understand that impact is to keep a diary of whom you have called and then observe their reaction to you the next time they see you.

Even those who are not celebrating a special day like to be checked on from time to time. If you make just one short "greeting" call a day, you can positively impact 365 people in a year.

We will address email later in the book, but using the web for simple greetings works well too. You don't have to write anything lengthy, just a note that says you miss a person or are thinking of them. Still, a greeting in person or a call always seems to carry more weight.

Embracing Greeting As a Life-Changing Habit

All of us can think of examples of people who use greetings to lift our spirits. We all can point to these warm people and tell others why they make us feel so special, but are we emulating them, or are we just standing back and letting them do the work?

During my son's first visit to the campus of Ouachita Baptist, a bright, energetic young woman lit up the room with a smile, a firm handshake, and a manner that said, "We are thrilled you are here!" Was Heather Sanders busy that day? You bet. But she was not too busy to greet someone who might fit in at OBU. With her first hello, Heather won Rance over. As they walked the campus and Heather greeted others in the same manner, my son knew he had found the place where he wanted to spend the next four years of his life. Because of Heather, I felt great about the school too.

You create your first impression on a person with the way you greet them. If you are happy and you show it, and you continue that type of warm greeting every time you run into that person, you have established a foundation for your words to make an impact for a lifetime!

How much better would our world be if everywhere you went people smiled and tossed a sincere hello each other's way? You can start the ball rolling and help create a wonderful world filled with great smiles and positive greetings by embracing this practice right now. Who knew a simple hello could have so great an impact?

5

I Don't Know
What to Say

In the late spring of 2007, my wife learned that her aunt
Cindy had terminal cancer. Cindy was just nine years older
than my wife and had always been more like a sister to her
than an aunt. Even though Cindy had fought breast cancer
two years before, the news came as quite a shock, for the
doctors felt that she had beaten it. Now, having recently
retired and having just entered her sixth decade, with
three grandchildren and a fourth on the way, a husband of
forty years, and two adult sons, this beautiful woman was
informed that the rest of her life would be numbered in
weeks, not decades.

As my wife and I contemplated this report, I was reminded of the fragility of life. Cindy and her husband, Jim,
had invested wisely and had been planning to visit all of the
places they had dreamed for decades of seeing. And they
were both on top of their game; just a week before she was
told she was dying, Cindy had played her best round of golf
ever. But suddenly, with no warning, Cindy's world shrank to

her bedroom in the family's home. In a matter of weeks, the cancer would evict her even from this comfortable refuge.

Over the years, I saw Cindy only at occasional family get-togethers. And as time had gone by, those reunions grew rarer and shorter. So except for observing her big smile, noting her quick wit, and witnessing the incredible job she and her husband had done raising their boys, she was really a stranger to me. Yet in the last month of her life, I grew to know her very well, not by speaking with her but through the actions of others.

Cindy did not face death alone. Scores of people came to her home, bringing food, books, meals, and conversation. These friends of all ages sat by her bedside and shared memories that suddenly became as fresh as the days they were made. Cindy smiled, she laughed, and she cried a bit, but most of all she realized how much she was loved and how much her life and words had impacted others. Her death was easier because those she had touched in life had the courage to face death with her.

I Wouldn't Know What to Say

So many times in life I have used the excuse, "I wouldn't know what to say." Rather than visit a grieving family or a sick friend, I would take the easiest route out and tell myself, "I shouldn't go because I just wouldn't know what to say." I have come to realize that this thinking is simply cowardly.

None of the more than one hundred people who went to Jim and Cindy's home knew what to say either. But that did not keep them from coming by, making phone calls, or sending cards and emails.

Most of us will find ourselves in many situations in which we don't know what to say. I have found there is generally only one thing you can say that is worse than staying away and saying nothing: "I know exactly how you feel."

None of us knows exactly how anyone feels when they are going through a tough time. If we have lost a spouse, we might be better able to identify with Jim, but each relationship is really different, as is each tragedy or loss.

I have never had cancer or lost a wife, parent, or child. I had no experience to pull from to help me come up with something to say to Cindy's family. So what could I say? On the surface nothing, but when you get to the heart, there is so much to say and so many reasons to share.

Admitting Your Ignorance

I have found that the first and most important thing when dealing with a tragedy is admitting that you lack the words to make things better. Words cannot change events. And in any case, changing what has happened is not what you as a friend have been called to do. So what do you say? The best way to begin is to be honest and admit, "I have no idea what you must be feeling right now, but is there anything I can do to help you?"

That might sound trite, but the reaction you will receive is likely to be much better than if you began the conversation with, "I know just what you are going through." Nine times out of ten, that statement produces a nonverbal response that means, "No, you don't," and makes the rest of your words meaningless.

So begin by being honest. Don't offer hollow words, but rather be sincere in your desire to help.

Think before Speaking

Most people going through a horrific disease or trying to recover after a great loss are in a state of shock. Often buried in their sadness is anger. Even people of great faith usually question why this terrible tragedy happened to them. So in the hours and days after the bad news has come, those doing the comforting must use their heads before opening their mouths.

I've known few people who ever found reassurance in hearing, "This is a part of God's plan." These seven words usually trigger one of two reactions. The most common is anger. The emotions of those trying to make sense of a tragedy are fragile enough without having to deal with thoughts of a supreme being whose plan includes randomly zapping wonderful loved ones. The other reaction is to become incredibly depressed that the God they worship has chosen to use disease or death in his mighty plan. Maybe a few months or years down the road they will be able to see something good come out of this event, but for the moment, nothing good or divine is in it. They are at a loss as to how God can use it.

Words That Break Fragile Hearts

Even worse than saying, "This is a part of God's plan," is the statement, "You must have done something to bring this on. You need to get right with God."

Years ago, noted speaker and bestselling author Marilyn Meberg faced the loss of her young child. Her baby had been born with spina bifida and died just two weeks after her birth. Joani's death plunged Marilyn into a seemingly bottomless state of depression. During this time, some of her friends actually "comforted" her with "This is a part of God's plan." As you can imagine, those words hurt a great deal and helped not at all.

Seeking answers, Marilyn went to a pastor for counseling. This man told her, "You lost your daughter because God is punishing you for something that is not right in your life." Imagine how those words cut through Marilyn's heart. Consider the guilt and pain that were added to her suffering.

Marilyn and her husband were the ideal Christian couple. Nothing they had ever done could have caused God to lash out at them. Still, for a while Marilyn, now consumed with guilt, took careful inventory of her life, trying to find the place where she messed up so badly that her Lord would take her child. Trying to spot her own shortcomings made her grief even worse. Marilyn didn't begin to heal until a much wiser and more compassionate pastor stepped in and gave her advice that led to real understanding.

None of us speaks for God, so let's not embarrass him by acting as if we do.

Listen before Reacting

Being uncomfortable usually creates two different verbal responses. One is to clam up and say nothing. The other is to prattle on and on. One of the most important things you can do when dealing with someone who is going through a tragic experience is to listen.

Once you have admitted that you don't know what to say and have offered to help, step back and wait to hear what the person has to say. Most people who are upset or confused don't want to be alone. What they really need is a sounding board, someone they can talk to. And when given an opening, they will talk.

I have found that when dealing with a death, it helps to remember the good times. Saying something that evokes a warm feeling or a memory can help lighten the moment. The critical thing is to listen and pick up on what direction the grieving person seems to want to go. Then gently say something that will take you down that path with them.

Being Scared Is Normal

No one wants to deal with death or disease. Most people would rather run in the other direction than talk to someone who is facing trouble. But remember, even though you don't want to deal with a tragedy, the ones who have been hit by it need to know that others care. So even when instinct tells you to run, this is one time when you need to hold your ground.

I was at a loss to know what to say to Cindy's sons during the funeral. I was honest enough to admit that to Jeff and Mike up front. Then, rather than add a trite throwaway line, I listened. Later, after I had observed how deeply these boys loved their mother and how many others did as well, I finally found something I could share with them. My words were simply, "You all are feeling so much pain because of the love you shared. Your sense of loss must mean that the bond between you and your mother was deep. It was so deep because she gave you so much of herself and her time. In that sense, even though you have lost her, you are so much more fortunate than those who mourn a person they wish they could have known but never did. A lot of parents and children never have a bond, and death only heightens this fact and makes the pain of missed opportunities all the greater. What I saw in Cindy's life and what I see in your love for her means she was an incredible mother, and only a blessed few know that kind of love. I am sure you will take what you learned from her and share it with your own children. You will be a better parent because of your mother's example, and your children will come to know your mother in your actions."

These words came after several hours of observation and were sincere. I could not have faked them. At the time

I said them, I had no idea if they really came through as I had intended. Only later when one of the young men sought me out to thank me did I come to understand that I had given him something to hang on to. Of course, my words were not really what made an impact; they were just a reminder of the incredible impact of a mother's love.

So when dealing with someone grieving a loved one's death, share a memory, talk about how that person touched you and others, be honest, and ask if there is anything they need done. If you do this in a sincere fashion, you will be a comfort to them during their worst of days and will also help lead them to better days down the road.

Don't Quit Talking

The days following a death usually bring a fairly large outpouring of sympathy. People send flowers and cards and make calls. Being surrounded by friends and family helps a grieving person make it through this tough time. For many, the support stops after the loved one is buried. But that is probably when real friendship is needed the most.

Don't quit calling, don't quit writing, and don't assume that enough time has passed. No one really ever fully gets over the death of a loved one. So accept the responsibility of being the one who is there after everyone else has left. If necessary, give yourself reminders to make sure you keep up your support. Listen to the grieving person's stories; as time goes by, the memories will come flooding back and they will need to share them. Most important, do whatever it takes to make yourself available. If you do, you will have the opportunity to make a great impact with the things you say.

A Friend Indeed?

While dealing with a death is difficult, visiting with someone who has a serious disease seems even harder. I once heard a doctor say, "When cancer strikes, people flee." When a person is diagnosed with a serious disease, many friends quit calling or coming by.

None of us likes to get hurt. None of us enjoys the pain of great loss. When we have a friend who is facing a deadly disease, we often run the other way to avoid the sense of loss we will feel if our friend dies. Yet by avoiding that friend, we are burying them before the fact. And if they do live, they will wonder where we were when they needed us the most.

Another illogical reaction to a serious diagnosis is that some people seem to fear catching the disease themselves. If the illness is communicable, this might make some sense. But most potentially fatal diseases aren't communicable. This fear is little more than an excuse that allows us to avoid confronting what really scares us: the fear of not knowing what to say.

Just Be There and the Words Will Come

So what do you say? First and foremost, you know the person and you know their personality. You should relate to them as you always have. Recognize that they have fears and that what they need the most are people around them who really care.

When my wife's aunt was in her final weeks, she immensely enjoyed the visits of friends and family. What she seemed to relish the most was reliving old stories. These memories, heightened by sharing them with those who were there, brought more laughter than tears. It also seemed to illustrate to her that she had lived a rich life filled with a great many blessings. But maybe most important, the visits of friends and family allowed Cindy to have the support she needed when it most mattered.

When a person is sick, the true depth of a friendship is revealed. The ill have both physical and spiritual needs, and someone who is not afraid to get involved can use this experience as a way of thanking their friend for all they have done. And the person battling the disease realizes that something that they did or said made a difference to their friend and had real impact. Knowing that provides strength.

So what do you say? The same things you always said. Don't change your personality or the way you relate to the person. What they need more than anything else is someone who has the courage to be herself. And if the opportunity avails itself, find a natural way to remind them of the many special things they have done for you, what your friendship means, and how they have inspired you.

As my wife helped tend to her aunt, she not only enjoyed being able to give back to her but also was deeply enriched through her visits with Cindy's husband and children. They each shared the important stuff of life, creating a bond that will be there as long as they each are alive. In sharing this great loss, those who rallied to Cindy's side found themselves being comforted even as they reached out to comfort Cindy.

Forgotten by All but One

There are homeless people all over the world who once had scores of friends. For many of these homeless men and women, a tragedy struck and shattered their lives. In many cases, when they were suffering the most, no one had the courage to reach out and help them. The lost rarely ask for help; it's our job to make sure we see their pain and respond to it.

In 1741, on a lonely London street, a physically broken man lived in fear for his life. Though he was barely middle-aged, a series of strokes compounded by rheumatism made George look much older. He was also almost blind. So his world, which had once been in such sharp focus, was now little more than a blur. Worst of all, he owed far more money than he had, putting him in danger of losing his tiny, rundown house on the wrong side of the city.

This man had once been famous and fabulously successful. He had once claimed friends in every level of society and was on a first-name basis with the British royal family. But as his business dealings suffered, his so-called friends abandoned him. George soon discovered that without money, he really had no friends at all. In failure, he was all but alone.

With no one to talk to, this creative man wallowed in self-doubt. Logic told him that when no one stepped forward to embrace him, his life was essentially over. The only thing left to answer was whether he'd spend the rest of it alone in his tiny home or in the cell of a debtors' prison.

With so many bills due and no way to pay them, George dreaded the mailman's knock. He felt sure there would never again be any good news in his life. Yet on a warm day in August 1742, the sick man received a letter written by an old friend. Initially, George was shocked that someone cared enough to write to him. With his eyes filling with tears, he held the envelope as if it were a thousand pound note. Little did George know that this letter would not just change his life but would still be rocking the world two and a half centuries later.

The friend who penned that letter, Charles Jennens, was a wealthy eccentric whom most folks avoided. Those who knew him labeled his behavior as bizarre. He always seemed to have a new idea to do something a bit differently than anyone had ever done it before, and none of his ideas ever panned out. So any letter from Jennens would have been dreaded by most who knew him. Few would have even bothered reading the note. But George opened the envelope with a rare zeal for a sick man, encouraged that at least one person on earth had not deserted him.

Excited and thankful, George grabbed a magnifying glass and anxiously read the words written by a true friend.

After the customary greetings and news of his family, Jennens wrote that he had been trying to write a musical, but that he had hit a wall. Try as he might, he simply couldn't do justice to his idea. Charles thought George might be better suited to finish the work, so he was asking for his help.

As he explained in his letter, Jennens had taken what he felt were the most important biblical stories centering on the Messiah and cut them down to what he viewed to be the essential passages of Scripture. His goal had been to create a new musical presentation, but he simply didn't have the talent to complete it. Maybe, he thought, old George would be interested.

George was not just interested; for the first time in years, he was inspired. His inspiration came not just from the Scripture Charles had collected but in knowing that someone still believed in him and felt he was a man of great value. On August 22, George locked himself in his study and set to work. In seven days, he created the first segment of his new musical. The next part took nine days. And the final piece took another week. After reworking the music several times, George felt the new oratorio worthy of sharing with an audience. That opportunity came when another friend wrote asking George to conduct a charity concert.

When a down-and-out, forgotten, dismissed, and all-but-homeless man named George Frideric Handel premiered his *Messiah*, the world again took note of the great composer. That work, inspired by a letter, saved Handel's life while giving the world one of its greatest musical expressions of joy, hope, and love. While it's Handel's work we now remember, it was the words of a friend, Charles Jennens, that first made the impact.

You Have to Be There to Make a Difference

During the brief final weeks of Aunt Cindy's life, scores of friends had the courage to go through the last lap of the race with her. Why did so many turn out for this woman? Simply because she had once gone the extra mile for them. When they were going through trials, she was the one who called or came by for a visit. She didn't let not knowing what to say keep her from reaching out. And invariably, by simply going and being there, she found some way to convey that she cared.

So even if at first you are stumped about what to say, being there is a good start. The words will come to you as you become comfortable enough to relax. Most of all, you will be rewarded in so many different ways for your effort, courage, and compassion. By getting sincerely involved in helping people during their greatest need, we will assure ourselves that in our times of greatest need, when we need words of impact from someone else, they will be there for us too.

6

The Importance of Expressing Emotion

On March 4, 1993, on national television, Jim Valvano was presented with the Arthur Ash Courage Award. His body riddled with tumors, the forty-seven-year-old man struggled just to move to the podium to accept the award.

Valvano first grabbed the spotlight by coaching a national championship team at North Carolina State University. Later, he became an honored basketball analyst. But this would be Valvano's last moment in the public eye. Though he hadn't prepared anything to say, he confidently stepped onstage one final time. And in his brief unscripted remarks, he delivered words that impacted tens of thousands on that late winter night and have since touched millions.

"I'm fighting cancer; everybody knows that," he said. "People ask me all the time about how you go through your life and how's your day, and nothing is changed for me. As Dick said, I'm a very emotional, passionate man. I can't help it. That's being the son of Rocco and Angelina Valvano. It comes with the territory. We hug, we kiss, we love. And when people say to me, how do you get through life or each day, it's the same thing.

"To me, there are three things we all should do every day. Number one is laugh. You should laugh every day. Number two is think. You should spend some time in thought. And number three is, you should have your emotions moved to tears, could be happiness or joy. But think about it. If you laugh, you think, and you cry, that's a full day. That's a heck of a day. You do that seven days a week, you're going to have something special."

In his speech, Valvano showed that life is not about titles or awards; it's about being fully engaged. Those who allow themselves to laugh, to think, and to cry are never afraid of showing their emotions. In fact, they embrace the chance to feel, and they freely display the ups and downs that make up their daily lives.

Is Laughter the Best Medicine?

We are drawn to those who always seem to be in good humor. Go to any gathering of a large number of people and observe those who are most popular in the group. Most of the time you will find that people who laugh easily are the ones at the center of the action.

Long before he was a successful coach, Jim Valvano was a very funny man. He charmed people into listening to him not just by sharing humor with them but by tapping into their funny bones as well. Essentially, he lifted people up because he saw the world as a wonderful place. A lot of others feel their lives are great, but for some reason they cannot let their emotions come to the surface. Not only does this cheat the world by denying it a few more upbeat moments, but it can affect your health too.

Several different highly regarded medical studies seem to prove that the old saying "Laughter is the best medicine" is right on the money. When Jim Valvano prescribed laughing, he was actually giving sound medical advice.

But Valvano's formula for a full day didn't stop with laughter. It also included crying, which we know is also a great stress reliever. But beyond the positive effects that expressing your emotions can have on your health, think what it can mean to others. Being honest about all of your emotions opens the door for others to feel. Your openness and comfort level with your feelings create an atmosphere in which others want to know why you were so moved. What had they missed that you observed or felt?

We Start Life Ready to Partake of Our Full Emotional Menu

For a healthy baby, the world is a place where emotions are freely expressed. An infant has yet to hear the unwritten rules of society that say you should always keep your emotions in check. When a child is happy, you know it because they show it. When they are frightened or upset, that's easy to spot too.

I have seen stoic adults, men and women who never let their guard down in public, get caught up in the emotions freely shown by children. When they hold a baby in their arms, these serious individuals are suddenly grinning, talking in gibberish, and doing all kinds of outlandish things to entertain the little one. And when this happens, freedom and joy fill a room.

Contrast what you have observed in the interaction between healthy, happy, and loved children and their loving parents with what you see in many third-world orphanages. In certain former communist-block nations, children's homes are filled with infants who never smile or cry. They lie silently in their beds, staring into space. The overburdened staff that tends to these children feeds them and changes their diapers but never holds them or expresses any positive emotions to these little ones. These children grow up in a world void of all laughter and tears, a colorless world that is so sterile, no emotional seeds are ever planted, much less grown. Thus these children are robotic in their reactions to all the stimuli around them and are completely detached from the world. Most never escape the emotional void that consumed their formative years.

Though most adults aren't as robotic as abused children in third-world orphanages, they nevertheless do everything in their power to stifle their feelings. For some reason, many believe releasing laughter or tears is a sign of weakness. They hide what they feel from people around them. Not only do they cheat themselves of many of the beautiful highs found in life, but they also prevent others from being impacted by those things too.

The Courage to Share

In the summer of 2007, *Good Morning America*'s popular cohost Robin Roberts revealed to the world she had just found out she had breast cancer. Roberts was honest about her fears. In the days before she was scheduled for surgery, she spoke not from the head but from the heart.

"At first I thought, 'This can't be. I am a young, healthy woman.' Neverthless, I faced my fear head on and made an appointment to see the doctor." She explained the nature of her discovery and added, "So in the coming months, you will probably notice that I will have my good days and my bad days, but I know I will get through it with the love and support of my family and friends.... I can't stress enough how important it is to get screened and checked for all cancers.... I am so blessed that I found this in the early stages."

Robin's emotional approach struck a chord with people. Within minutes of her tearfully telling her story, message boards were bombarded with responses. People who were fighting the disease drew courage from Robin's faith. Even though they didn't know her personally, they felt they had found a sister in their struggle. Others, who had previously ignored warning signs about cancer, headed to their doctors for a checkup. Even giving to cancer research went up in the days that followed the broadcast. Robin's public display of emotion during a trying time prompted positive action by thousands of people.

You don't have to have a television audience, have a large fan base, or be fighting an illness to share from your heart. The best place to start is with your family and friends. There are many in that group who need to be inspired and motivated by your honest emotions. Don't be afraid to admit your fears and freely share what brings you the greatest joy. By doing so, you can impact people through your experiences just like Robin Roberts did. In the process, you might save a few lives and give others a reason to live. Most of all, you will not be alone.

The Prime Minister of Humor

Grady Nutt was one of the best speakers I ever heard. A dynamic preacher, he was once called the "Prime Minister of Humor." Never have I heard a man who could bring passages of Scripture to life as he did. In the often black-and-white world of Bible study, he gave characters a third dimension—emotion—and packed his stories with color.

Grady painted interesting pictures of men and women who were struggling with the problems of their day. He gave these characters personality, then wove that depth into his lessons. Suddenly you could feel the shame of the woman at the well, see the compassion and forgiving spirit of Jesus, and sense the mob mentality of those who were disgusted to be in the presence of sinners. In his hands, these stories were no longer flat or static; they took on depth and illustrated the courage it takes to stand up for forgiveness when the world is asking for retribution.

Grady's gift was bringing real emotion to all of his stories. In Grady's Bible, there was laughter. His humor, often making fun of his own shortcomings, helped underscore the lesson. His emotions put into motion a place where everyone could identify with him and his subject.

Lasting Value

It's no accident that the movies and television programs that remain popular long after they have ended are the ones that make us laugh. *I Love Lucy* will probably be entertaining millions of people fifty years from now. The same is true with the likes of *The Andy Griffith Show*, *M*A*S*H*, and a handful of others. At the core of these programs was making people feel better through laughter. Yet under the grins that each show produced was usually a subtle message too. Like Grady Nutt's use of humor, there was always a point.

When you consider the people who have made a great positive impact on your life, what they have in common is their ability to share their emotions, especially humor. We all treasure the teacher whose great lessons were wrapped in humor. We feel blessed to have friends who speak words that lift us up rather than tear us down. Being surrounded by these kinds of influences makes us more positive about our own world.

If you want others to look to you as an inspiration and to be positively affected by your words, then set that in motion with positive emotions.

If You're Happy and You Know It

Saying what's on our hearts is the purest form of emotion. It's what children always do before we start teaching them to keep their emotions inside. I'm still not sure why that unwritten rule has become so much a part of culture. Instead of instructing children to hold things in, we should encourage them to share their feelings with all those in their lives. There is an old song, "If You're Happy and You Know It." If you want to impact others' lives, put the spirit of that song into action. And nothing brings happiness like knowing you are loved.

I am an only child, but I have been blessed by a close friend who decided more than thirty years ago that she was going to be my sister. As this sibling relationship developed, I discovered she displayed her emotions much more freely than I did. When she felt something, she didn't assume I knew it—she told me. I could never end a phone call or a visit with her until she said, "I love you."

I genuinely love a lot of people in my life. Yet beyond my wife, I have never been very good at actually stating that fact. When this "sister" told me she loved me, she always waited for my response, so I was forced to say what I really felt. Over time, articulating my love for people became much easier. I even took the lead and told others I loved them before they said it to me. Most important, I no longer just assumed that people knew how I felt.

I now think about how tragic it would have been if I had not told my grandparents how much I loved them. I know they knew it through my actions, but I am sure it meant much more to them to hear me say it. During their last years, they had full confidence that they knew what they meant to me. So thanks to my "sister," you don't have to guess if I love you. I tell you.

Putting Your Emotions into Action Words

In the winter of 2007, Linda Cunningham was suffering from severe headaches. Within minutes, a brain aneurysm put her at death's door. For weeks, she barely hung on. Then, just when it appeared she was getting better, a second aneurysm ruptured, and her family was called in to say their farewells. Yet Linda refused to die. Instead she rallied and fought through the second attack on her fragile body. After months of hovering between this world and the next, she began to put her life back together.

Linda's brain had been badly injured. Among other things, she had to relearn how to read and write. As she began this process, she discovered stacks of cards that had been sent by her many friends when she was in a coma. Inside many of those cards were heartfelt messages describing what Linda had meant to their lives. Longing to read these tributes, Linda went to work on her therapy. In time, she made a full recovery.

One of the keys to the speed of Linda's comeback were the messages in those cards. The words kept her going, made her realize she was loved, and provided her with the motivation to continue to inspire all those around her. She still keeps those cards for times when she feels down. Just reading them offers an immediate lift!

If You Are Emotionally Honest, It's Easy to Make an Impact

A midwestern grocery store brought in a consultant to suggest how they might create more business. She advised the employees to find ways to put a personal stamp on their jobs. If they did that, the customers would connect with them in a special way, creating a loyalty factor that would generate more sales for the store.

Most of the employees barely even listened to the consultant's advice, but a nineteen-year-old bag boy took her words to heart. Johnny had been born with Down syndrome, and though he loved his job, he wondered how he could possibly do something that would make a lasting impact on the store's customers. After considering what made him feel better, he opted to find or create a thought for the day. Working with his father, Johnny created a short, positive message on the family computer, printed those words onto small slips of paper, and began placing one of "Johnny's Daily Thoughts" into each customer's bag.

A few weeks later, the store's manager noted that one of the checkout lines was four times as long as all the others. He raced over to the back of that line and pointed the customers to other registers where there was no waiting. Each person refused to move. They informed him they were waiting in lane three because that was where Johnny was bagging, and they wanted his thought for that day.

Johnny's words were an honest emotional gift from a caring man's heart. Many customers who had come into the store once or twice a week were now shopping every day that Johnny worked. And it was all because of what he was giving to them.

Inspired by the bag boy, other store employees soon came up with ways to personalize their service as well. Special wishes such as, "Get well soon, we miss seeing you," were put in prescription bags, and flowers with broken stems that would have been tossed in the trash were turned into corsages and given to senior citizens who passed by the floral counter. Johnny's thought became a movement that was even taken to the company's other stores.

To this day, Johnny creates daily inspirational thoughts, and it has given him a new sense of value. No matter his supposed handicap, he realizes he has the potential to positively affect others. His expressions of emotion have richly impacted his customers, and it took only a few minutes each day. Each of us can use our words in a similar way.

The Simple Steps of Sharing Emotion

1. If you love someone, tell them. Don't assume that they know how you feel. Treat each opportunity as if it's your last chance to express your love for that person.

2. If you send a card to someone you care about, write a short note explaining why you love or respect that person. Once again, don't assume they know your reasons; explain them. Those personalized comments might well be the words they need to take them through a hard time or to lean on when they try to accomplish something special.

3. Don't be afraid to reveal your emotions. You will miss more than you know by hiding them. If you are happy, show it! If you have to, sing the old song each morning to remind yourself to share your happiness.

4. If tears come, let them. Crying makes us all human while also making us approachable. Don't run away from things that make you cry. Cherish movies and television programs, songs and stories, and even old memories that move you to tears.

5. Say what's on your heart. Embrace the emotions you find inside of yourself.

6. Finally, be happy and allow your happiness to show. See the world as a child would, and get giddy over the simple joys. Don't stifle laughter!

Negative Words Are Like Bombs

Several years ago, I was at a high school basketball game watching my oldest son play. The officiating that night was well below par. As the clock ticked and I observed the refs making more and more mistakes, my attitude changed from one of a joyful parent supporting his son into one of an angry member of a mob. By the third quarter, I was up on my feet screaming at the men in stripes. Soon my voice grew so loud that people started to look at me. I had supplanted the game as the center of the action.

Later that night, I began to understand that my negative emotions had done a great deal of damage to my standing. I looked crazy, and who is going to take a crazy person seriously? I also looked stupid, and who is going to listen to a stupid person? And finally, I was obviously raging with anger, and who is going to be drawn to an angry person?

We cannot ignore the fact that hateful words and emotions can do just the opposite of positively influencing others and lifting people up.

Consider the politics of hate and fear. It relies on the mob mentality. It shuts people out rather than inviting them in. It divides people rather than bringing them together. It destroys rather than builds up.

Just as someone's words influenced Abraham Lincoln to feel compassion and seek to end oppression, another person's words inspired Adolf Hitler to hate and kill. How do we avoid being the voice that inspires anger?

Take Ownership of Your Attitude

You don't have to allow anger to control you. You don't have to give in to the negative forces in your life. In fact, it's pretty easy to embrace an attitude that puts you in the light-filled corner rather than the dark one.

1. First recognize when your attitude is changing. When I got mad during the game, I was allowing outside actions to determine my reactions. That's how rage usually works. We don't act; we react. Pause, take a deep breath, and realize how you will look if you "lose it." Consider the damage that might be done.

2. If you are using words to put people down, then you are not lifting others up. For a moment, put yourself in the place of the person you want to verbally tie into, and you'll usually find that there is a better way to approach the situation. Remember the Golden Rule.

3. Remember, just as it has been medically proven that being happy and laughing increase your life span and improve your health, anger and yelling have been proven to take a huge toll not just on emotions but on your health as well.

4. Always picture the way you want to be remembered. Few of us want others to remember us as the angriest voice in their world.

5. Consider what negative emotions and words do. It was anger that fostered the attacks on September 11, 2001. It was anger that drove the Ku Klux Klan. It was anger that fueled Nazi Germany.

6. The most important way to be a positive influence is to remove the negative influences from your life. If you are surrounded by people who are filled with anger, you really need to find other people to be your friends. If you discover that your negativity is fueled by what you are listening to on the radio or watching on TV, change the channel. If your music is depressing you and causing you to voice negative emotions, ditch it.

Don't Ever Give Up

Jim Valvano realized that life is simply too short to waste it in anger. Even when his body was wracked with pain, he felt a great need to enjoy each moment. At the end of his final speech, he thanked ESPN for helping him to set up the Jimmy V. Foundation for Cancer Research. He explained that the motto of the organization would be, "Don't give up; don't ever give up."

Then he added, "And that's what I'm going to try to do every minute that I have left. I will thank God for the day and the moment I have. I'm going to work as hard as I can for cancer research, and hopefully, maybe, we'll have some cures and some breakthroughs."

He concluded, "I said it before, and I'm gonna say it again: Cancer can take away all my physical ability. It cannot touch my mind, it cannot touch my heart, and it cannot touch my soul. And those three things are going to carry on forever."

A few weeks after he accepted the Courage Award, Jim Valvano died. Yet his positive message lived on. In fact, the organization he started for cancer research developed treatments that have saved thousands of lives, including that of Jim's own daughter Jamie. Now that is impact!

Life Is Too Short

Life is fragile and it is short. The days we have to make an impact are not as many as most of us imagine. Few have gone to the grave saying, "I wish I had taken more time to be mad." Few have gone to their grave saying, "I wish I had told more people how much I hated them." Most people have faced their last days wishing they had said "I love you" more often. Most have also faced their final days wishing they had been more open with their positive emotions and more often revealed their true self to the world. They wish they had acted with more childlike joy.

If you are not laughing and smiling each day, it's time to take the mask off. It's time to put away the fear of revealing your love and toss the anger and grudges in the trash. It's time to positively express yourself and, in the process, lift up those around you. If you hitch a ride on a smile, you'll be surprised how many people will want to travel with you down life's road.

7

Paying Attention

Most of the great lessons I have learned in life have come from standing back and watching or listening to other people. One of my most profound out-of-the-classroom educational experiences took place backstage after a concert. The example given to me on this summer evening continues to influence the way I treat others.

In the 1980s and early 1990s, Barbara Mandrell was one of the most popular and charismatic entertainers in show business. Her high-energy productions, unbelievable talent, and singular ability to connect with every audience placed her at the top of her game. Her drive and effort ensured that anyone who bought a ticket to watch her perform got more than their money's worth. Hard work drove her to stardom, but it was her ability to continue to wow fans that kept her there. Yet as great as she was on stage, her off-stage performances were even better!

One night after a concert at the Grand Palace in Branson, Missouri, my family, along with scores of other persons, many of them very wealthy, powerful figures, was invited backstage to a reception hosted by none other than Ms. Mandrell. I'm sure that after singing and dancing for more than two hours, Barbara was exhausted, and certainly her status as a superstar meant that she didn't have to mingle with fans after a performance. And yet on this night, she addressed this task with seemingly as much enthusiasm as she had brought to her show.

As she made her way around the green room, she smiled and visited as if she were hosting an intimate party for good friends. At the time, my youngest son, Rance, was no more than six years old and spent most of his time at the reception standing in a corner watching everyone mingle. When Barbara spotted the small boy, seemingly very much out of place in the crowd of adults, she grinned and slowly approached him. As I watched, I was immediately taken in by three things she did.

First, a smiling Barbara knelt to put herself on Rance's level. When she was eye to eye with him, she reached out and lightly touched his arm. And finally, as if he were the only person in the room, she asked him a question. For the next few minutes, it was simply Rance and Barbara. She was all his.

When she and my son concluded their conversation, Barbara gave him a hug and moved to another person, this time an adult, using almost the same technique to connect. Her smile, her eye contact, and the light touch of her fingers assured the woman Barbara was talking to that what she had to say was important to the superstar.

I noted that as Barbara continued to work her way through the room, she similarly made each person she met feel as if they were the only other person in the room.

Not all of us are comfortable reaching out and lightly touching others. Yet after her smile and opening question, Barbara used touch to assure those she was talking with that she cared deeply about them and was concentrating on what they had to say. Touch and eye contact were the singer's way of connecting with those who had come to see her.

Barbara's Lessons Applied

When I was first pushed by publishers into making personal appearances at bookstores, I felt incredibly uncomfortable. Finding myself in a room with a group of people I had never met, I initially wondered how I could relate to them. Most of the time the patrons were as hesitant to approach me as I was to greet them.

Then I remembered Barbara Mandrell's example. Looking each person in the eye, I stuck out my hand, smiled, and said hi. Then I asked, "Where are you from?" Almost always from that point forward I not only had started a great conversation but also had found a new friend.

Over the years, I have come to realize what Barbara sensed during her brilliant career. As people, we all have a great deal in common, so starting a conversation with someone, saying words that count enough to draw them into the moment, is pretty easy. All it really takes is a bit of work with your eyes and ears. A quick glance at any individual provides you with a pretty clear snapshot of who they are.

Rules for Meeting and Greeting

1. Find something to compliment. Everyone has something that you can say positive things about. It could be their eyes, their smile, their hair, what they're wearing, or maybe you can tell that they work out. After your greeting, extend the compliment, opening the door for them to enter into conversation.

2. Make eye contact and keep it. This makes a person feel as if you want to hear from them. People will warm up to you if they sense you are interested in them. By focusing on that one person, not allowing your eyes to dart around the room, you will go a long way toward creating a bond.

3. If the conversation dies, ask a simple question. Asking where someone is from opens the door for a myriad of follow-ups. If you note a wedding ring, you can ask about their family. One simple question usually tears down the walls of hesitation and shows your interest in their life.

4. Even if you are in a meet-and-greet situation, as Barbara was, make sure you leave that person with a sincere word of thanks for spending a bit of their time with you. Your goal in any conversation

should be to make someone else feel as if they are of great value. If you accomplish this with the way you react to people, you will make a mighty impact.

Putting the Other Person First in Your Family

Gloria Gaither is one of the most successful songwriters in the history of American music. The gospel music tune-smith has enriched and impacted countless lives with her words. What started her on this incredible trek to international acclaim? What gave her the foundation for feeling that what was on her mind and heart had value for the entire world? These questions cannot be succinctly answered, but the woman's path was probably set in motion by something as simple as dinnertime at her family home.

Gloria's parents believed in education, but they also believed in using what their children learned to challenge their thinking. At supper, all distractions were set aside—there was no radio or TV playing in the background—and as the family sat around the table and shared a meal, they spoke not just of the day's activities but also of what they had observed, experienced, and learned. If Gloria had been reading a book, then her father asked her to share with the family what she had gotten from it. If she had been in a play or contest, she spoke about that. This sharing didn't end with books and school programs, either; it included friends, music, sports, and anything else family members had encountered that day.

Gloria's friends were drawn into her home by the family's love and warmth. Hence the house became a gathering point for kids from all over the community. When her friends ate with Gloria, the family made them feel just as important as blood relatives.

In Gloria's case, this parental care went beyond the table. If the family was going someplace in the car and someone had something to say, the radio was turned down and the conversation took center stage, placing a high degree of importance on each family member's thoughts and words. This stopping the world to hear someone else's thoughts showed great respect as well as engendered self-confidence. Both of these important elements provided the foundation for Gloria's accomplishments later in her life.

Rules That Signal Respect

In many families today, there is no quiet time. The TV is always going, the phones are always answered, and the music never stops. It seems that words are everywhere, but few of them are our own, and when ours are spoken, it's hard to hear them over the din of the electronics that dominate our lives. As a result, the generations are growing even farther apart, talk is cheap, and fewer deep bonds are made. It's little wonder that kids and parents often don't respect each other's opinions. How can you expect anyone to respect you if they are always having to shout to be heard?

In a recent CNN poll, teens were asked what they treasure more than anything else. The majority answered that it was time with their families. So in giving kids their fondest wishes, create an environment in which people can bond. To give your words impact at home, as well as to uncover thoughts and encourage dreams, here are some simple things you can do:

1. When someone is trying to talk to you, turn off the TV or radio, put down the iPod, set aside the computer, and after everything is quiet, look at them and listen.

2. Show you are listening by responding to what they are saying. Ask follow-up questions or at least give a response that indicates you understand the importance of this information. Ask questions and wait for answers.

3. Don't hurry them. If they want to drag it out, allow them to do so. Don't look at your watch or the clock. During important conversations, time doesn't matter.

4. Think about what they are saying before hurrying back to your work. Even after they leave the room, pause to consider what you have learned.

5. If you can't stop whatever it is you are doing at that moment, at least take a second to explain

that you will spend time visiting with them as soon
as you finish what you're doing. Then make good
on that promise.

Tune Out, Then Tune In

Riding in the car is a great time to visit. We have a habit
in our family that we always begin each trip with the radio
off, inviting conversation. I am convinced this has created
an environment in which our sons have felt that their words
are really important to us. I know that my wife and I recon-
nect on every trip, short or long, thanks to the quietness of
our rides.

You can tell if someone is really putting you first on the
phone. It's not only a distraction but a slap in the face if
background noise is blaring through the receiver. It simply makes you feel as if you don't matter. If someone calls
you on the phone, mute the TV or radio, quit doing things
with your hands, and pay attention to each word they say.
It usually helps you concentrate if you picture the other
person as if they are in the room with you. Don't just talk to
them, but see them too.

As a writer, I do a lot of radio call-in shows. I am usually
in my office with my phone in my ear as callers ask their
questions. For me, this is kind of like taking an oral exami-
nation. So I listen carefully to every word each caller says.

This is the same kind of attention we need to give
everyone who calls us on our private lines. Treat that
call from a friend or family member as if later you will be

quizzed on what is said. Doing so will place you in the heart of the conversation, show that you believe the caller to be the most important person at that moment, and provide a forum for you to learn and share. You are giving that person the same respect you would give them if they were sitting at your table.

If you really are too busy to talk at that moment, if you have an appointment or work you can't put down, then explain that to them and give them a specific time when you will call them back. And make sure you do call them back right on time. I know of at least one person who badly needed to find someone to talk to; several people put her off, and when no one called her back, she killed herself. So follow up on your promise as if a life depends on it. Most times it doesn't, but the call probably will make that person's day much brighter.

If you are in public, consider what Barbara Mandrell did. Find a way to give that person your complete attention. Even with the noise and activity around you, signal that you are hearing only them. If you have to, move to a hallway or the corner of the room. Don't let distractions take your mind off the person speaking to you.

The key to showing respect in conversations is making sure that the other person feels like they are the most important person in the world at that moment. So no matter where you are, tune out the world and tune in the person who asks for or needs your attention.

Observation Is the Sign of True Caring

We are often guilty of concentrating so hard on what we are doing that we don't notice anything around us. This singular vision can be misread as aloofness. It's hard for people to listen to you if they feel you are usually ignoring them.

For many years, Becky McGee was my contact person at my bank. In spite of the fact she was one of the busiest people I knew, she always found time to smile, to give a warm greeting, and to ask about my life. When I told her things, she remembered them and brought them up again the next time I saw her. When I asked her about banking issues, she gave them her full attention. Yet in my dealings with her, I always felt that I was much more important than closing the deal. Because of the way she treated me, long after she was transferred to another branch of the banking chain, I stayed loyal to the bank. And I still feel that if I have an issue that needs to be addressed, Becky will still be interested in helping me.

The way I feel about Becky is the way all of us want others to feel about us. So in our dealings with people, we must make people feel as if our time with them is the most important thing at that moment. The bottom line is that we must never be too busy to make another person feel special and never be so caught up in our own world that we don't see others around us.

When I was in college, Barbra Streisand had a popular song called "People." The chorus embraced this wise thought: "People who need people are the lucki-est people in the world." At first that might sound a bit strange, but when examined more closely, that refrain presents us with the essence of why we should always put the people in our lives before everything else. We need them. Without people who care for and depend on us, we are lonely and have little value.

So we need people not only to help us accomplish the things we do each day but also to provide us with the wisdom to get through the tough times of our lives. If we treat the people in our lives with respect, if we give them our time and focus, we have a much better chance of their listening to our words and giving us an open door to express our own thoughts.

How Valuable Is Your Time?

No matter what your religion, there can be little argument that Jesus Christ's life and words have affected more people than anyone else's who ever lived. His time was precious: he had only thirty-three years on earth and had a lot to accomplish during that time. Yet when you examine writings about his life, they don't dwell on the things that seem to matter most to us in our modern world. Try to find a description of the way he looked or how he dressed. Evidently Matthew, Mark, Luke, and John didn't believe these details were important. At least they didn't waste any space on them in their writings. What they did capture was the way Jesus treated people.

Consider the woman at the well or lepers. In the view of everyone in his company, these people were beneath Christ. The culture of the time said that he shouldn't have given them the time of day. Yet he didn't just acknowledge them; he took the time to speak with them. His words assured them that they were important. As his words changed their sense of their own value, they also changed their lives.

As you go through your daily life, are you more like Christ, or like the citizens who watched him? Do you shun those who don't fit into society's definition of importance, thereby putting them down, or do you stop and lift them up? Jesus stopped everything in his world when someone approached him. He showed respect to those who asked for a bit of his time and attention.

Stop, Look, and Listen

When I was in college, I visited with Grandma Collins every chance I got. She was by then a widow, in her eighties and living by herself. She had many grandchildren, but little money, so she couldn't take us on trips, buy fancy presents, or give us money. About all she could give us were her time and her advice. The former was given liberally; the latter was given subtly.

Whenever I went to visit with Grandma and the weather was pretty, we would wander out to the carport that she used as a covered patio. While sitting out in the fresh Arkansas air, she and I would talk. I would tell her all about my life at school, my friends, and my dreams. She would listen as I rattled on about how I was going to change the world. In time, she began to chime in with stories about her own life at my age, even working in a few lessons she learned along the way. During those visits, when there were no distractions and chores were put aside for a while, I gained a great deal of insight into the most important things in the world, little lessons I later used as I raised my own children. As I look back on those moments, I realize that a woman who was nearing the end of her life made a large impact at the beginning of my life by sharing stories that emphasized the value of humor, honesty, and compassion. I learned that the best way to change the world is by listening and talking to one person at a time.

Fame and Fortune

One of the blessings of my profession is that I get to spend time around many people who are considered famous. I like to sit in the background and watch as seemingly sensible, normal people approach these celebrities. If they are fortunate enough to gain an audience with them, the fans usually hang on to every word that the star says, squeezing any possible meaning from each inflection and comment. I have seen this kind of adoration over and over again. I have also had many people repeat to me something a celebrity told them twenty years before. They remember the words as if the visit were just a few hours ago.

One celebrity I had the chance to meet was Ronnie Milsap. The blind singer was once a struggling musician who often sang backup vocals at recording studios to pay his bills. One day when he was in a studio waiting for another session, he sat down at the piano and began playing and singing an old Elvis Presley hit. Every note that came from his mouth sounded like a solid impersonation of his musical idol.

After listening to Milsap for a few minutes, a man strolled over. Waiting for the music to stop, the stranger gave the singer a compliment, then added, "But with all your talent, you should quit trying to sound like Elvis and just be yourself."

This advice jump-started a great career. Later, Ronnie found out that it had come from Elvis himself.

The kind of attention fans pay to stars provides each of us with one of the best examples of how to take part in a conversation with a friend or family member. Hang on to each word, imprint on your mind each sentence, and reflect on what that person is sharing with you. And most important, treat that person as if they were the only soul on earth at that moment. If you do, there is a good chance they will hang on to what you say as well, and some of the advice you share with them will make a lasting impact.

Like the Last Time

One of the keys to keeping yourself focused on the person who is talking to you is to keep one question in mind: what if this were the last time you ever visited with this person? If you had been given that information ahead of time, you would no doubt pay much more careful attention to the conversation and try to speak words that have real value. For all of us, there is a last time and a last word, so by living every moment as if this were that moment, our lives and the words we use will have greater impact.

In certain areas, Barbara Mandrell and I are much different. Our views on politics, reading, movies, TV, and even food will never completely mesh. Yet my respect for the way she treated those who came into her world overrides any of those things that set us apart. Why is that respect there? Because whenever I was around her, she always gave those she met that same kind of eye-to-eye attention. She did this no matter their age, position, or social status.

A dozen years after my son spent a little quality time with Barbara, he still remembers the way she treated him. He also now employs the lessons he learned from that meeting in his dealings with his friends, family, and professors. Even though he was just a child, Barbara's way of saying her words had a great impact on his life. This is one example we can all take to heart and put into practice to make our own impact on others.

With family, friends, and even those you don't know, the best way to set a foundation for making an impact is to respect others enough to tune out the rest of the world and give them all your attention. As they grasp how important their words are to you, what you say will mean much more to them.

8

Sharing a Word

One of the things we cherish most in the world is good news. What many of us don't realize is that news doesn't have to be earth-shattering to be shared. It's the little things that often make the deepest and longest impressions.

Julie Belyea is a good friend of our family. For years we have gone to church with Julie, and together we have watched our kids grow up and graduate from high school. Julie has one of the most incredible smiles of any person I have ever met. It starts not on her lips but deep in her heart—totally and completely sincere. I always look forward to seeing Julie because I know that I am going to see that warm smile as well as listen to her share something joyful with me.

Julie's natural manner of sharing good news was planted in her heart by her grandmother. Julie's grandmother lived just across the road from Julie's mother and father. These were rural Texas people who had little but their modest home. Julie's grandmother didn't even own a phone. Yet whenever Grandma got something special in the mail, she couldn't wait until the next family gathering to share it. To let everyone know the postman had brought good news, she always grabbed a big cowbell and shook it as fast as her tiny arms could move. Everyone dropped what they were doing to come to Grandma's and share in the joy.

One of the things Julie and her grandmother both understood was that good news splashes over, landing on others and lifting their spirits as well. Whether they are communicated through email, snail mail, phone calls, or face-to-face conversations, positive thoughts shape not only your attitude but the mindset of everyone around you. If you keep things upbeat and sincere, your communication will not only be pleasant; it will probably always be uplifting. So if we care about others, it's vital that we share good news.

Actions Are Your Loudest Words

Several years ago, I observed an older man who always came into our church services after the musical part had ended and the pastor's message was just beginning. For years I figured the reason for Milton's tardiness was that he just didn't like music. It was only after I had done a bit of research on the man that I learned a great lesson about love and devotion.

Milton had been married for more than fifty years. Most of those years had been happy and normal. He and his wife had created a successful business, raised two children, and enjoyed the changes that are part of going through life hand in hand. But as she entered her senior years, Mrs. Wright's personality dramatically changed. Medical tests revealed she had an aggressive form of Alzheimer's disease. Unable to take care of her growing needs, Milton was eventually forced to place her in a nursing home.

The nursing home suggested to him that it would be in his best interest to divorce her. She no longer knew him, and if she had no husband, the state would pick up the tab for her care. Though it would have saved him tens of thousands of dollars, Milton refused to go this route. He would not turn his back on the woman he had loved for so long. So each day, Milton went to that facility to have breakfast, lunch, and supper with a woman who had no idea who he was. During those meals, he continued to share with her the joys of their life together. Milton was late to church simply because he always had a breakfast date to keep.

Milton's words during those meals meant little to his wife. She couldn't comprehend who he was or understand what he was trying to share. But his words and actions spoke volumes to all who witnessed their meals together. This great lesson in life went beyond devotion and vows. Because he continued to share good news with his wife, many others understand that it's not so much what we say that matters; it's the spirit in which we say it.

As a basketball fan, I watch a lot of games on TV and in person each year. I have been to the state of Kansas only once and have no affiliation with Kansas State University, but in 2006 I first watched a freshman point guard toss her body all over the court for her team. She didn't give an inch, pushing harder than anyone on the floor, and yet, in spite of this exhausting effort, a real joy was written on her focused face. I was so impressed by her can-do spirit that I started to follow her team.

I soon discovered that Shalee Lehning gave everything she had every night she played. My family was so wowed by her efforts during televised games, we went to watch Shalee play in person. Amazingly she always seemed to exceed her talent level and perceived potential through massive effort and desire. Her game was always grow-ing! We weren't the only ones who noticed how much she gave. After every game, scores of kids followed her around, and this college star always took the time to make each of them feel special. She was a magnet for young and old alike, all because of the way she spoke through her at-titude and effort.

As we visited with those who had known her for years, we discovered the real reason so many lionized this young person. Shalee tried as hard to live up to the highest moral and ethical standards off the court as she did on the hardwood. In the classroom, through her Facebook page, through all the other areas of her social experiences, Shalee knew the eyes of the world were on her, and she was moved to reflect the image of Christ to those who watched her in each of her pursuits. That spirit is what put the smile on her face and the drive in her actions.

Our attitude and effort always speak volumes and make a huge impact on more people than we can imagine. They draw others to us. Best of all, we all can do this. Neither age nor vocation can limit our ability to give everything we have in each of our public tasks. Milton and Shalee understood this kind of devotion to life and blessed others simply by living it daily.

Why Share Good News?

None of us ever accomplishes anything alone. It is always a "we" triumph. Therefore, those who have been a part of creating the joy need to share in it as well.

In the world of entertainment, acts come and go as quickly as the seasons change. Few manage to stick around more than a few years. One of the groups that lasted is the Statler Brothers, who stayed at the top of their craft for decades. Why did they last so long? One of the major reasons has to be the fact that they never held themselves above their fans. In fact, they put their fans on a pedestal.

The Statlers understood that it's the people who buy the tickets and recordings who are the bosses. The group realized that essentially they worked for these people. Without them, they would have been nothing but another struggling act. Consequently, the Statlers shared their successes and all their good news with their fans. Each gold record, award, and honor was another reason to celebrate, and that celebration always included everyone who had been part of making it possible. This included not just the fans but their elementary school teachers, Sunday school teachers, record producers, and even those who had the courage to book them before they were famous. Every bit of good news was a chance to have a "we" moment.

If something worth sharing happens in your life, remember it happened because a lot of other people supported you when you were down and out or struggling. Share the joy and make sure those with whom you are sharing understand that they helped make this wonderful thing happen.

Knowing What to Say

A friend of mine is a UPS driver. One day, Carl was given a billfold that had been found along his route. Finding the owner's address inside, Carl arranged to meet with the individual to return the wallet.

At the meeting, Carl met a frantic teen, who anxiously opened the wallet. The boy was shocked to see the several hundred dollars he had placed in it still there. After counting his hard-earned money, the teen looked up at Carl in disbelief. He had obviously expected at least some, if not all, of the cash to be gone.

Needing to get back on his route, Carl shook the shocked young man's hand. Almost as an afterthought, the boy said thanks and asked Carl if there was anything he could do for him. Carl smiled and answered, "Just remember that someone took the time to find you and was honest in their dealings with you. When you have the chance to react in the same way, please do so." Did Carl's actions make an impact? He will never know, but his parting words at least were a positive charge that might have given the boy something to think about. It also might have changed his whole life.

Simple Rules for Sharing

1. The first step is showing that you actually care and that you are sharing the information because you feel this person is important to you. People can look right through fake sincerity, but the real thing runs deep. If you really care, they will see it in your eyes and hear it in your voice. So don't share unless you really care.

2. Don't call to brag; call to share. The difference between the two will be immediately recognized by others who are listening to your words. If you are including the other person in your joy, if you are thanking them for being a part of it, then they will respond in a positive way. If it seems that you are trying to lift yourself above them, it comes off as haughty.

3. Think carefully about who you share your good news with and remember it is a "we" moment. If they can't be included or would miss the sense

of joy, if this is something that they won't identify with or appreciate, then it's best to pass on making that call. But if they really care about you, if they have invested in your life, then don't hesitate.

4. Always find a way to enlarge the spotlight to include the one with whom you are sharing the news. Milton's wife couldn't understand what he was saying, but everyone else understood that Milton was sharing his good news because he felt his wife, through her many years of love and support, had made it possible.

5. Most important, when someone calls you with good news, you need to be as excited about it as if it were your own. So make as big of a deal out of the triumphs of others as you do your own.

Share Your Joy

There are so many ways to share your good news with others. The most obvious is either by visiting face to face or making a phone call. But joy can be wrapped in all kinds of packages, and depending on the relationship you have with another person, you can use any or all of them.

1. Face to face. For some people, it's hard to share good news face to face. If they see someone while out in public, they hold off sharing something special. By doing so, they miss an opportunity to make an important connection in life. Remember, sharing your own good news opens the door for

others to share their good news as well. If you make it a point to ask others for updates on their job, family, or hobbies, you give them a chance to share something with you. Sharing good news also builds a bridge that can be used when people are going through tough times and need someone to lean on. By opening up on the little joys in your life, you might have a chance to make an impact down the road on matters of great importance. When my son received an academic scholarship in college, I immediately shared this news with his teachers. They were thrilled to know they had been a part of it. By the same token, I didn't brag to others whose kids had not been so blessed.

2. Telephone. Phone calls are an immediate way to share the good news. The same rules apply as with speaking face to face, and the same rewards await you when you share. Again, don't be shy; if someone cares about you, they will revel in your joyful moments too.

3. Email. The third easiest way to share joy is through email, but it's also the way most likely to be misused. Be careful how you use this wonderful tool. Don't send good news out in a blanket manner, but carefully choose whom you share it with. Reread your email several times to ensure that the note carries the good news with the humility that will allow it to be taken the way you intend.

Remember to make it a "we" moment, including the receiving party and giving them some credit for this wonderful happening.

4. Mail. Using the postal service can carry great rewards for you and those who receive your message of joy. Because a letter takes time to write and costs a bit of money, the person who reads your letter and learns of your news in this manner will likely feel as if they are special. If you want to make a huge impact, sending the news in a letter is often the best route to take.

Joy Can Be Created, Then Shared

All over the globe, few images bring universal joy like Santa Claus. Santa is one of the world's best "feel good" characters. Why does he almost always make us feel wonderful? It's not just because he gives; it's also because he is so happy to be giving. To understand the full impact of this icon, you need to understand his DNA. Santa wasn't just invented; he sprang forth from the joy shared by two different men.

In the fourth century, Nicholas of Bari was born into a rich family in what is now Turkey. His parents died when he was in his teens, and a mourning Nicholas turned to his faith for comfort. Feeling called to use his wealth to help the poor people of his community, the young man gave away his riches and dedicated his life to reaching "the least of these." His mission evolved into bringing joy into the lives of needy children everywhere he traveled. Dressed in the red robe of a cardinal, Nicholas touched thousands with his generosity during his life—and has touched millions since.

In the early tenth century, another teenager lost his parents. The Duke of Borivoy lived in an area now known as Bohemia. By birthright he became the leader of his kingdom when his father died, and he ruled with a compassionate hand rarely seen during this period. Like Nicholas, the duke was driven by his faith and the need to share it. Each year, on the night before Christmas, he trekked through deep snow, knocking on the doors of the poorest families and distributing food, clothing, firewood, and toys. Today we know this man as Good King Wenceslas.

Nicholas and Wenceslas were the men who inspired the creation of Santa. In spite of tragedies in their lives, they each found a way to uncover joy and share it with others. Essentially whenever Santa says, "Merry Christmas," or whenever a poor child is given a gift through a charity program, Nicholas and Wenceslas are still touching lives and living out their positive calling. Their impact is even stronger now than it was when they were alive.

Finding Ways beyond Words to Share Your Joy

There are limitless numbers of ways for each of us to share joy through actions that speak louder than our words. The joy felt through this kind of work can impact even people you will never meet.

1. Every area has charities that need volunteers. One telephone call can usually get you connected to an organization that can use your positive impact. Find one that fits your personality and your interest. If you are passionate about your mission, your joy will show in your words and actions.

2. More and more schools are looking for mentors. The pressing demands of modern education mean that teachers need help, especially in reaching children who have learning problems. Your impact and words can serve as inspiration for a student. Tens of thousands of kids owe their college degrees to people who gave them the extra help and motivation they needed in elementary school. This is a great way for your words to make a lasting impact.

3. Habitat for Humanity and similar organizations give you a chance to help build something of lasting value for a needy family. While you work, your words can also make a statement to others about how important sharing joy is to you.

4. Churches are in constant need of volunteers for building projects, food programs, and other community outreach services. Working with these

programs speaks volumes about your passion for spreading joy to others.

5. Scouting, YMCA, and recreational programs give you a chance to get involved in sharing words that can shape lives forever.

The list of places that need you is endless, but if you go where you are *really* needed and where you can really be yourself, you will have the opportunity to share your joy, and later your words of wisdom, with many people. When you give from your heart, the joy pours forth!

Seeing Joy in Others and Telling Them What You See

None of us ever fully knows the impact of a simple gift of time, a smile, and a positive word. By pointing out the joy you see in someone else's life, you might well be uncovering something they overlooked. Finding joy or the potential for joy in others is a way for your words to make an impact.

Several years ago at a church gathering in the Midwest, an older couple was seated at a table with a middle-aged blind couple, Janie and Steve. At first, the sighted members of the group were a bit uncomfortable. They constantly caught themselves avoiding words like "see" or "look." For a while it appeared the evening was going to be a disaster, yet as there was no other choice, the older couple tried to keep the ball rolling.

During the course of the conversation, the older couple discovered Steve had only recently lost his sight, but

Janie had been blind for many years. Out of curiosity, the sighted woman asked Janie if she had ever seen Steve. Janie smiled, leaned forward, and whispered, "No. Why? Is there something I should know?"

The sighted woman was taken aback by the question, but before she could think of a reply, Janie laughed and added, "Just kidding. I don't have to actually see him to see his love."

Not only did the reply break the ice, but it began a friendship that spanned years. And it all started with a bit of humor.

Another story of a blind person underlines the importance of a positive word at the right time. In the middle of the darkest days of the Vietnam War, a young man from rural Missouri was badly injured and lost his sight. Gene had grown up in a world where his father constantly berated him with negative comments. He told his son that he was void of talent, worthless, and destined to be a failure in everything he did. These words took root, and by the time he was in junior high, Gene came to reflect his father's viewpoint.

Now lying in a bed unable to see, the twenty-year-old man sensed his life was over before it had really begun. If he was worthless when he had 20-20 vision, then surely he was without value now. He probably would have continued in this frame of mind for the remainder of his life had it not been for the message of joy he found in a solitary voice.

There was a nurse on Gene's ward at the VA hospital who sang out as she entered his room. This woman struck up a dialogue with the lonely man and shared with him all the wonderful things she saw in him. Over time, the nurse convinced Gene he was handsome, bright, and talented. Building on the traits she observed, she convinced him he could do anything he dreamed of doing. The nurse's sincere words persuaded Gene that he had great potential. In just a few weeks, she erased a lifetime of doubts and inspired Gene to continue his training to reenter the real world. Once there, he obtained his undergrad and graduate degrees and became one of the most successful homebuilders in St. Louis.

So not only do you need to share the joy that comes into your own life, you also need to find it in others and convince them of what you see. Your observations might well inspire them to great things.

Joy's Bright Light!

One of history's most quoted and beloved speeches was given two thousand years ago by a man known as Jesus. It's most often called the Sermon on the Mount. Many elements of this profound message have great lasting impact, but in thinking about this chapter on sharing joy, what is written in Matthew 5:15–16 really stands out: "Don't hide your light! Let it shine for all; let your good deeds glow for all to see."

The old children's song "This Little Light of Mine" presents a similar message. Allowing the joy in your heart to burst forth in words and allowing others to hear your good news opens a door for others to share things with you. If you look for and see the potential for light and joy in others, you receive an opportunity to inspire and lift them as well. And when you share and see joy, you establish a foundation of friendship that you can draw on during the trying times that hit all of our lives.

So don't be shy. Ring the bell, light the light, and share the joy in your life with others. And always be open and excited when they share their joy with you!

9

Positive Coaching

Over the years, I have had the honor to work as a volunteer in several Special Olympics competitions. The contestants in these events never cease to amaze and inspire me. In a wide range of events, they push themselves to do their very best, giving much more effort than I generally see from kids competing in school events at field days.

Yet the best part of this experience is what I see from the coaches and fans. No one is screaming at the officials or coaches, no one is verbally abusing the participants, and no one seems to be in a bad mood. A positive aura envelops everyone. Maybe this is because at the end of each event, every participant is made to feel like a winner. Those waiting along the finish lines are there to give both praise and hugs to reinforce this concept. All that is required of those competing is the will to do their best.

For many decades, Communist China refused to admit that there were any mentally retarded people in their nation. Those suffering from such afflictions as Down syndrome were hidden away and never given a chance to claim even a small spot in a dim spotlight. It was as if they had never been born. Even years of pressure from Western nations didn't change China's view of the developmentally disabled.

But what government leaders around the world couldn't change, the testimony of the Special Olympics finally did. The international exposure created by these true "goodwill" games made such an eye-opening impact that the leaders of China began to quietly organize their own competitions. In 2007, the veil hiding millions of wonderful Chinese was lifted when the Communist nation threw open its doors and hosted the International Special Olympics. Consider this for impact: the volunteers who serve Special Olympics all over the globe, whose main job is telling each contestant what a great job they did just by competing in an event, accomplished something that the leaders of the most powerful nations could not.

When you consider this dramatic effect, you have to wonder why this teaching approach isn't used in every sporting, educational, and business setting. Positive coaching almost always seems to work as both a motivating tool and a confidence builder. Yet even in the face of such dramatic success, many seem to believe that yelling and screaming is the only way to get people's attention and provoke change.

A Negative World

Turn on the TV or radio and you are often hit with a wide variety of negative images. This is true not only of the news but of entertainment as well. Unlike the days when television programs stressed the right way to do things, few programs today dwell on presenting positive images. Talk radio also seems to center on destroying people rather than building them up.

Why did we change from the positive to the negative, and how has that affected our views, actions, and even our words? Most claim that it's all about ratings. They tell us that the ranting and raving, the violence, and the sex are what people want to see. If that were so, why do so many tune in to programs like *Extreme Makeover: Home Edition* each week? I think viewing and listening choices may be based more on the fact that the country is sinking in a sea of cynicism.

If you are surrounded by negative attitudes, you will become a negative person. If everyone around you is looking for the worst in others, then you will too. If you are in a confrontational world, then your words will be confrontational. Your environment shapes your actions and words.

Imagine a Special Olympics where everyone screamed and yelled angrily at the participants. What if only the first-place finishers were praised and the rest were degraded as losers? The athletes, instead of feeling exhilaration, would feel anger, frustration, pain, and anguish. They would believe they are of little value to anyone.

It's no different in the real world.

What Positive Words Can Do

Kate was just ten years old when she sang at a war-bonds rally during World War I. The featured speaker at that event was General John "Black Jack" Pershing. The commander of all the American armies was so taken by the little girl's strong voice that he took her to the White House, where she performed for President Wilson. The president embraced Kate and urged her to use her incredible talent to bring people joy for the remainder of her life. Little did Wilson know that his positive charge would sustain Kate through some very dark times.

When Kate graduated from high school, her parents begged her to go to nursing school, but remembering the president's words, the young girl traveled to New York City to try to carve out a niche on Broadway. People were still wowed by her voice, but it was her size that got her work. Kate was a very large woman, weighing well over 230 pounds. She often had to take jobs with comics who poked fun at her girth. In time the negativity almost caused Kate to give up on her dreams. Yet President Wilson's words of praise sustained the woman through those horrible days. It was the one thing she really had that sustained her belief in herself.

In the late twenties, a well-known talent agent happened to catch a show Kate performed in. Ted Collins was so impressed that he set up an appointment to visit with the young woman. Self-conscious about her size, Kate all but apologized to Ted when they met. But the agent wasn't interested in her figure; he wanted only to find a way to display her voice. First Ted convinced Kate she could be a star. Then he introduced her to a medium in which her voice was all that mattered. In 1931, with Ted Collins's positive words pushing her all the way, Kate Smith became the most popular star on radio.

Wilson's and Collins's encouragement and praise kept Kate Smith from giving up on her dreams, and their words carried with them a great spillover effect. The bubbly singer became a radio favorite. She was also the embodiment of the American dream, a woman who overcame great odds to become a star. As a result, she inspired many others who were downtrodden during the days of the Great Depression. For thousands who had almost nothing, she was the sunshine that helped them make it through a very dark period in their lives.

In the late 1930s, Kate found an Irving Berlin song that the great composer had rejected two decades before as not being up to his standards. She put her own spin on Berlin's "God Bless America," and the song quickly became a national institution. Within three years, Kate and this patriotic ballad would undergird the morale of millions during the most trying days of World War II. Six decades after it first aired, Kate's version of "God Bless America" still inspires today.

Few of us realize the great power of our words. When we lash out with them, we have no way of knowing the effect they will have on the object of our attack. Many a person has been destroyed by thoughtless verbal assaults. Yet when we use our words as President Woodrow Wilson did, to lift someone up, ultimately millions might benefit from that positive encouragement.

Finding the Positives

Louise Mandrell has long been one of my best friends. Anyone who has seen her on stage knows her incredible talents as an entertainer, but let me assure you that she is an even better person. She lifts people up rather than tearing them down.

From time to time, Louise and I work on projects together. I have even had the pleasure of helping to script some of her shows. On several occasions, I have given her material that she didn't really like, but she never came out and directly told me that I had failed to please her. Instead, she carefully went through all of the material until she discovered something she thought had merit. Latching onto that element, she began our discussion by praising that part of the script. Her compliments buoyed my confidence and revved up my energy reserves. Then, after I was really enthused, she dropped the hammer: "The rest of the script shows promise, but it simply doesn't come up to the level I found here. I want people to see your best work, so I have a couple of suggestions that we might be able to use in these other places that seem weaker than the part I am thrilled with."

Often I found myself reworking more than three-quarters of a script, but because of the way Louise verbalized her critique, I never minded. I never once felt like I was under attack. So even when she was disappointed in what I had done, she found a way to make me feel good about my efforts and want to work even harder. That is positive coaching at its best.

In the 1996 Summer Olympics in Atlanta, Kerri Strug became an unlikely hero. Strug had struggled with so many injuries throughout her career that many had written her off before the games. Even after she made the American team, she was overshadowed by her more publicized teammates. When the team competition for the gold medal came down to the vault, the feeling was that the title would rest securely in American hands even before Kerri made her jump. But disaster struck when one of the darlings of the games, Dominique Moceanu, fell on both of her attempts. Suddenly, the only hope for a US team gold medal rested on Strug's shoulders.

With her coach Bela Karolyi looking on, Kerri made her first jump. Things looked good until she landed awkwardly, wrenching her ankle. In pain, Kerri limped down the runway for her second attempt. In those moments, few expected her to be able to complete the run, much less make the jump.

The audience cheered its encouragement as Strug studied the distance she had to cover. During these moments, the voice of her coach could be heard saying, "You can do it, Kerri! You can do it!" Karolyi continued to yell those words as the young girl gingerly tested her ankle. Finally, with Bela continuing to express his belief in her, Kerri raced down the runway, flew into the air, and did the impossible, sticking a perfect landing on only one foot. She held the pose the necessary time to complete the event, then collapsed.

Until this moment, Bela Karolyi was generally known as a gruff coach who constantly pushed his pupils. Yet because of his upbeat reinforcement at the 1996 Olympic Games, this bear of a man will always be remembered best for yelling the most positive message anyone can hear: "You can do it!" This kind of positive coaching always seems to have the greatest effect.

We Are All Coaches

Most of us will never pick up a whistle and coach a team. But that doesn't mean we're not coaches. Almost all of us do that job even if we don't have the title. We are constantly coaching our kids and grandkids, as well as our spouses and even our friends. Coaches motivate others to learn, so teachers are coaches. So are Sunday school instructors and preachers. If you are a CEO or a foreman, you are a coach. In fact, it's hard to find anyone who doesn't coach in some way. The question is, What kind of coach will you be and will those who play for your team listen to your words?

I visited with several members of a college basketball team one evening, and the subject of coaching techniques came up. One of the players related an experience she'd had with a coach whose motivational technique was to yell. This coach felt that the best way to create great players was to find every flaw and use them to tear his players down. The player explained that for a few kids, this approach worked, but most others were either demoralized, their confidence destroyed, or, like her, quit listening to everything the coach said.

It doesn't take a scientific study to reveal that most people, especially kids, need praise to move forward in life. They need to hear when they are doing well before they are told how they are messing up. If you lift people up enough, they will be happy to listen to suggestions for improvement. If you are always tearing them down, their accomplishments will tend to mirror the pessimistic view of their coach.

About two decades ago, I was watching the Duke University basketball team playing a close game. At the end of the contest, one of Duke's star players, Christian Laettner, was fouled and sent to the line. If Christian made both free throws, Duke would win, but if he missed them, they would lose the most important game of the season. With the nation looking on, Christian missed both shots.

The game over, the teenager sank to his knees, tears welling up in his eyes. For an instant, he was alone with the knowledge he had let his team down. Then racing to his side was his coach, Mike Krzyzewski. Coach K. pulled Christian off the wood floor and began speaking to him. The teacher kept telling his young pupil that he would have other chances. Over and over, Coach K. told Laettner how much he still believed in him. With Krzyzewski's arm around him, Laettner left the court.

If his coach had taken a different tactic, perhaps leaving without saying anything or ridiculing the player for his shortcomings, Christian might have been destroyed by those two missed shots. Yet thanks to the positive words of Coach K., the young center managed to regain his confidence and was the force that led Duke to back-to-back national titles. Those championships made young Mike Krzyzewski a household name, but it was his little-noted positive words to Christian Laettner that paved the way for that remarkable feat. Even after all of his Hall of Fame success, Coach K. remains a man who always puts his players' needs before his personal goals—an emphasis that defines a great coach and a great person.

About two thousand years before Mike Krzyzewski convinced Christian Laettner that he could bounce back and reach greatness, Jesus had to do some positive coaching with one of his struggling disciples. When Christ told Peter that he was the foundation on which a new and great work would be established, it took the man by surprise. Peter never really saw himself as having that kind of strength. Yet the confidence shown by Jesus took root in the disciple, and when the time came for him to show great courage, he was ready to stand up and be counted.

Putting the Positive to Work

1. There are times when we all must face criticism. It's a part of growth. But using a negative outburst shouldn't be the first option; it should be our tool of last resort and rarely used. The old saying that you can catch more flies with honey than with vinegar is true of humans as well. If you want someone to listen to you, go with the positive.

2. Don't raise your voice each time you are making a point. There are times when you might have to yell a bit to get someone's attention, but if you do it all the time, no one will ever pay attention to what you are saying. When you speak softly, people lean closer to hear your words.

3. Find something positive to compliment before you point out a flaw. It's not that hard to uncover something good, so look for it. If all you do is point out the bad, you will be avoided like the plague by the very people you want to help.

4. When highlighting a mistake, draw an analogy from a mistake you've made in your own life. Don't set yourself up as being perfect. If you reveal some of your flaws and mistakes, you will appear more human and have a much better chance of

the other person identifying with you. If they identify with you, they will probably listen as well.

5. Teach with a sense of humor. We put a great deal
of pressure on children and employees to perform. If they always see us as gruff and unforgiv-
ing, then working with us is going to be a miserable experience for them. Sure, some people
achieve greatness in spite of constantly being put
down, but most success stories include positive
coaching from upbeat, loving people.

6. No matter what you say, don't let the one you are
speaking to feel as if you don't believe in them. In
the Special Olympics, every contestant is a winner
just for trying to do their best. If you keep that in
mind as you work with others, if you simply praise
them for doing their best, your words will become
a foundation for greater things than you can
imagine.

7. Remember that each of your actions and reactions
are opportunities to make a huge statement. If
Coach K. had been so angry and self-consumed
about the loss that he had walked away from
Christian, it would have spoken volumes about the
coach's lack of character. What do your reactions
and words say about you when you are "coaching"
your family, pupils, or coworkers?

8. Our words to others define us. So find a way to be
a positive coach; say five things that lift up others

for every one criticism you give. Don't jump on someone until after your words have shown that you care deeply about them.

My father was an incredible basketball coach. He understood the game inside out. He could teach anyone the skills needed to play hoops. Yet what made him a great teacher was his understanding that everyone is different. He got to know his kids, reading their personalities, and he adjusted his coaching style to each individual. He realized that some kids would fall apart if they were yelled at even once, so he tailored his approach. With some he was serious, and with others he joked. His varied style resulted in incredible individual growth and team results. Ultimately, he instilled the belief that every one of his players, if given the opportunity, had a good chance at success.

This approach carried over to the classroom as well. Using a technique that positively challenged kids to reach their potential, Dad was able to encourage a majority of his students to far exceed expectations. He accomplished this by adapting his teaching style to meet the needs of each of his students, and he never yelled at someone for being stupid. While only one of his players ever made it to the pro ranks, scores of them used the tools he gave them to be successful in the game of life.

Just like on a basketball team, you can have ten kids in a family and no two of them are going to react alike. So the challenge becomes understanding how to speak to them in ways that they will listen to. One of the best areas to focus on might be your memories of them as toddlers. When they took their first steps, you praised them as if they had just won a marathon. Though they might not admit it, teens and even adults thrive on this same kind of praise. The most important element of this praise is to make sure your words tell them you love them and you believe in them. Christ showed this to Peter and the world was forever changed. Follow this example and the odds of your making a positive change in the lives of those you love are in your favor.

I Believe In You

If there's a theme running through every sketch in this chapter, it's "I believe in you." That could be the motto of Special Olympics. It was what Bela was saying to Kerri; and it was the message Coach K. gave to Christian.

Anne Brooks had grown up in a negative home environment before being turned over to a convent. As a child, Anne felt unloved and unwanted. In the convent school, she discovered an attitude of service that so intrigued her she became a nun. Earning a degree in education, Anne found herself in a profession in which she was constantly coaching kids to become better. But just when she had gained her footing as a teacher, the nun's days in the classroom ended. Struck down by arthritis, she was forced into a wheelchair. For several years, her world grew smaller as others constantly pointed out to her all the things she wasn't able to do.

Needing to get back to doing some kind of direct work with people, Anne left her desk job at the school a few days each week to do volunteer work at a free medical clinic. It was there a doctor told her that her condition could be reversed and she could walk again. This optimistic man put feet to his words by pointing Anne in the right direction to obtain the medical care she needed to regain a bit of traction in her life and career. When she was again ambulatory, the physician came back with more positive words. He informed Anne she had the talent and brains to become a doctor. Unable to believe in her own abilities, the nun scoffed at the idea of going to med school, but the doctor would not leave her alone. He continued to show her ways that she could succeed. He forced her not just to listen to his words but to see his dreams. Soon a spark was struck in the woman's heart. In time, it turned into a fire, all because of one man's words of encouragement.

Today Dr. Anne Brooks runs the Tutwiler Clinic in one of the poorest areas of the United States. Her practice in the Mississippi Delta has done more than just heal the sick or patch up the injured; she has expanded the positive coaching she received by pointing out the potential and talents of each of those she serves. Many have gotten their GEDs, and some have obtained college degrees. A few have even come back to work with her. Thanks to positive words that revealed her belief in those she serves, a light of opportunity is burning for the first time in this area.

And it all started when one man saw great potential where others saw none and verbalized what he saw!

Positive Words Create Positive Actions

So many have been drawn to the Christian faith because of the positive nature of Jesus' message. He was all about doing things that made a difference. He was into healing physical and mental wounds, not pointing out shortcomings. He was a master motivator, a coach who didn't just talk about potential but employed great coaching techniques to give that potential a platform for growth. His techniques should be the model for all of us.

If we surround ourselves with positive forces and if we embrace the positive on radio and TV, then we have a much better chance of coaching others up. If we shut the negative junk out of our lives, we will have the opportunity to look at the potential of those around us. Seeing others in this new light will lead us to realize how our words can push them to accomplish great things. Something we say might be the key to a child's believing that he or she can live their dreams or to an adult's making the effort to fight through a stroke or take on cancer treatments. After all, a few hugs and a lot of cheers, not a lot of screaming and threats, opened the nation of China to embrace millions they had hidden away.

So when working with others, start with the attitude of "you can do it," and you will find not only that you will lift them up to things they imagined were out of their reach, but that they will lift you on their ride to the top. If you want to see a change in your home, your community, or your country, then change the way you "coach" those who are a part of your life. It can all begin with a few positive words that make a lasting impact!

10

I Was Wrong

In the summer of 1960, fifteen-year-old Brenda Lee took a song penned by Ronnie Self to the number one spot on *Billboard*'s pop music charts. "I'm Sorry" stayed in the top position for three weeks and remained in the nation's top 40 for more than one third of the year. While Brenda charted another thirty times in her incredible award-winning musical career, her lyrical apology remains her signature song.

In "I'm Sorry," Brenda pleads for forgiveness for a "wrong she has done." Her performance on this recording ranks as one of the greatest of that era; it was such a perfect marriage of song and singer that no major artist has tried to cover it. But Brenda's incredible interpretation aside, the likely reason the record sold millions of copies was because so many could identify with its simple message. After all, everyone has done something they were sorry for, but few have admitted it in as sincere a fashion as Brenda did on her hit release.

Most people have a difficult time coming to grips with their mistakes, not to mention saying the two words "I'm sorry" or the three-word follow-up "I was wrong." We usually avoid those phrases like the plague.

A glance through any magazine or newspaper reveals that rather than being a society of people who admit their mistakes, we have become a finger-pointing culture filled with people who are always trying to shift the blame. Those who admit they have made a mistake or wronged someone might serve up an apology, but they often add a qualifying comment to diffuse their guilt, hinting that they messed up because of something outside of their control. Few seem to want to embrace the Harry S. Truman philosophy of "the buck stops here." The fact is that none of us is always right, and we all need to admit it when we discover we are wrong. It's not only the right thing to do, but it's the only way we can be completely respected by our peers.

Too Proud to Say "I'm Sorry"

One of the best-known biblical parables involves a prideful young man who demands his inheritance, receives it, and hustles off into the world to live his sordid dreams. I have always had a soft spot in my heart for the young man's father, a person who had worked hard to give his family a solid life and future only to have his son turn his back on all that parental sacrifice. I can't begin to fathom how the older man must have felt to see his child walk away from the family home acting as if he had just been released from a long stay in prison. It must have crushed him to know the boy had neither the wisdom nor the experience to properly use the money he carried in his purse.

As the familiar story goes, the prodigal son took savings that should have lasted a lifetime and spent them in a blink of an eye. Where did his fortune go and what did he do? The Bible doesn't give us a detailed description of the way he spent his inheritance, but it doesn't take much imagination to believe the son probably went to the nearest big city and partied it away. We can also be pretty sure that during those days of high living, he was surrounded by throngs of well-wishers who claimed to be his friends. Yet when the money ran out and he found himself eating from a pig trough, those fast friends all disappeared. For the first time in his life, he was broke, alone, homeless, and completely humbled.

For many, the lesson of the parable centers on a young man wasting a fortune on sinful endeavors. But the story's real moral point comes from the way the young man returned to his home. He swallowed his pride, admitted his mistake, and offered to serve his father as a slave in order to prove his sincerity. The respect the son was shown at his homecoming was no doubt due to his asking for forgiveness and stating that he was sorry. It was his genuine "I'm sorry" and "I was wrong" that paved the way back to full acceptance.

Taking Full Responsibility

The prodigal took responsibility for his actions. He didn't say, "Well, I wouldn't have lost my money, but the games I was playing were rigged," or try to deflect his stupidity by saying, "Dad, if you had just told me what was out there, I could have handled it. It was really your fault because you didn't prepare me for the real world!" He didn't shift the blame. There was no qualification in his plea for forgiveness.

In the last few years, various government heads have become very good at apologizing for wrongs committed by others long before they came to rule. The Queen of England recently apologized to the Maori in New Zealand for things done hundreds of years ago; the Vatican apologized for turning a blind eye to the Holocaust; and the American government apologized both for enslaving African-Americans and for its treatment of Japanese-Americans during World War II. Yet these same governments still have a real problem apologizing for wrongs committed in the present. Most leaders never come close to admitting that they have erred. Judging by the careful language employed by spin doctors, you'd think the fault never lies with elected officials. In fact, even in the face of some of the biggest blunders in recent history, to listen to government officials, it often seems that no one really made a mistake at all.

Set against the grand scheme of history, personal apologies of the sort that Brenda Lee sang about seem to matter hardly at all. Yet just like the prodigal son, each of us has done things that have directly or indirectly hurt others. These wrongs have put us in a position where our words and actions have little impact on those who have felt the sting of our mistakes. So while we are often frustrated that the most powerful people in the world can't say "I'm sorry," are we ready to make things right in our own smaller worlds by telling our friends and family "I was wrong"?

Meaning It

The prodigal had been so humbled he had little choice but to beg for forgiveness. He did so expecting nothing in return. Yet he gained a great deal through his humbleness. In today's society, we are bombarded by celebrities, sports figures, politicians, and even preachers who call press conferences to tearfully say "I'm sorry." The list of their sins includes racial slurs, drug and alcohol abuse, and sexual liaisons.

Most of these apologies seem calculated to salvage people's careers rather than to signal a change in their ways. Most times these tearful pleas are qualified in an attempt to deflect some of the blame. Sadly, most aren't even sorry for their actions; they're only sorry that they were caught. Their words ring hollow and have little impact on the very people who have been hurt the worst.

Everybody Hurts Somebody Sometime

From time to time, even the best among us say or do something that hurts another. Often when this occurs, we either don't note what we have done or simply disregard it as insignificant. Yet saying "I'm sorry; I was wrong" can heal wounds, and healing wounds is the best way to forge a relationship of trust.

A few years ago, I took inventory of my life and thought about several people I had hurt in one way or another. In none of these cases did I mean to do harm, and certainly, by the world's standards, none of these instances were huge lapses, but nevertheless, because of the way I phrased my thoughts or reacted to a situation, I hurt or took advantage of someone. As a result, I had become smaller in their eyes, and from that time on, any words I spoke to them had less impact.

Pulling out a pen and some paper, I made a list of people whom I felt may have been hurt by something I said or did. Then I set out to find as many of them as I could and offer a sincere, unqualified apology. In most cases, I discovered my apology wasn't necessary, since no one's feelings had been injured, but in a few instances, I rebuilt bridges that had been taken down by my words or actions. In each case, my sincere humbling helped me gain a bit more respect, and that's vital if my words are ever going to have any value to those on the list.

In truth, making these apologies was pretty easy. It's harder to apologize to people who are closer to home—parents, spouses, and children. These are often the people who never hear a sincere "I'm sorry" come from our lips. We often assume this group knows how we feel, but since they are the very foundation of our world, they are the ones who need to hear us say these words each time we mess up. Divorces, rebellious children, and family splits have been the result of people being too filled with pride to admit they are wrong. If you want your children to be able to come clean with you, then you need to set the example. When you mess up, tell them "I'm sorry; I was wrong."

When my youngest son was in junior high, he and one of his friends became very rowdy while I was working to meet a deadline. I warned them several times to tone it down. Finally, the horseplay led to the breaking of an item so inconsequential I can no longer remember what it was. I verbally jumped on Rance, and when he tried to argue with me, I slapped him across the cheek. I was immediately ashamed of what I had done. Falling to my knees, I looked him right in the eye and said, "I am sorry; what I did was horribly wrong." He tried to take the blame for it, but I wouldn't let him. I explained that nothing he did justified my actions. Several times over the years, I have thought of that moment and gone back to Rance and again told him how sorry I was for that single slap. My stupid reaction could have torn us apart, but thankfully my expression of sincere regret brought us even closer together.

Putting "I'm Sorry" into Your Vocabulary

Studies have shown that "I'm sorry" and "I was wrong" are the two hardest phrases for most people to say. If you watched the old TV series *Happy Days*, you might re-member that the Fonz couldn't bring himself to utter "I'm sorry." He tried, but on each occasion the words just would not come out. Finally, when he did find himself in a place where he'd lose a close friend if he didn't apologize, tears came to his eyes and he whispered, "I'm sorry." This humbling action saved the relationship and opened the door for better things in that friendship.

Life is not a television script, but like the Fonz, we all need to put "I'm sorry" and "I was wrong" into our everyday vocabulary. And we should become so familiar with those words that they are no longer difficult to say.

Where to Begin

1. Recognize that you aren't perfect and that you make mistakes. If you can't accept this fact, you need to take a hard look at your life.

2. To get familiar with saying "I'm sorry" and "I was wrong," think about people in the past you may have hurt. If possible, find them and apologize. Beginning with those who are not closest to you makes it easier to apologize to those you see regularly. Apologizing is hardest the first time, but with practice, it becomes much easier.

3. Don't ever qualify your apology. It almost always makes it seem as if you're fishing for a good excuse for messing up. So forget the excuses and say the words that heal the relationship.

4. Be humble and don't act as if you're doing something monumental. Treat this as an opportunity,

not a punishment. Others, seeing your humility, will open the door for much deeper acts of forgiveness down the road.

5. Remember, rather than belittling yourself by admitting your failures, you are actually taking a step up to a higher plain. It takes a big person to admit a wrong, and this act will enlarge your stature. It will also rid you of verbal garbage that is keeping you from establishing stronger relationships with those around you.

6. Make it a habit to say "I'm sorry" as quickly as possible. Don't put it off or you will probably never do it. And if needed, say it more than once as you explain why it's important for you to apologize. If you really want to make an impact, after you apologize in person, put it in writing and mail it to the injured party.

7. Finally, realize that accepting your apology is up to the injured party. They might not be ready to forgive and forget. It's their choice to move on, and you have no control over anything but doing the right thing on your side of this two-way street.

Think Carefully before You Follow Others

History's most unfathomable crimes were usually incited by inflammatory words. Someone stirred up the hatred that led to Christians being killed for sport in the Roman arenas, women being executed in the Salem Witch Trials, the KKK lynching scores of innocent African-Americans, and the Nazis killing millions of Jews. None of these tragic events would have been possible if not for seemingly moral people getting caught up in the mob mentality and doing things that they would never do under normal circumstances.

If the situation is right, each of us probably could be inflamed into doing things we wouldn't normally do. Maybe you wouldn't ever find yourself involved in a lynching or the burning of a neighborhood, but you can probably still be influenced into actions that can hurt others and put you in a position to lose your impact on people who know you well. If you want to see this illustrated in a real-world setting, go to a sporting event and watch the crowd. You'll find gentle souls screaming for blood even at peewee football games.

If you do a Google search for famous attack speeches, you could spend the rest of your life reading them. If you do a search for famous apologies, the results probably won't take up more than a short evening of reading. Of the few recorded meaningful historical apologies, there is one that gives us insight into how careless speech can create the atmosphere for mob action.

In 1170, Henry II of England found himself locked in a struggle with a dear friend. Thomas à Becket was the archbishop of Canterbury and had long been a man whose word and wisdom the king valued. Yet over time, Becket stood his ground in matters relating to the separation of church and state. His unyielding nature deeply frustrated Henry's goal of influencing the direction of the church in both England and at the Vatican.

One evening, Henry sat by his fire and uttered these words to his most trusted friends: "Will no one rid me of this turbulent priest? What a band of loathsome vipers I have nursed in my bosom who will let their lord be insulted by this low-born cleric!" Henry was likely blowing off steam, yet Reginald Fitzurse, Hugh de Moreville, William de Tracy, and Richard le Breton interpreted his words as a call for brutal action. On Tuesday, December 29, 1170, these four assassinated Becket in the cardinal's church. One of those most shocked by this murder was the king. As he thought back on his conversation, he realized it was his careless words that had set in motion the horrible event.

Henry blamed himself for Becket's death, and in a step rarely taken by a member of the royal family, he publicly apologized to the church and to all of England. He even paid penance at Becket's tomb. Yet nothing he did could bring his old friend back.

My parents raised me to honor and respect others even if they are different from me. I am sure I often failed to live up to their teachings, but I remember the sense of rage that filled me when I watched kids in my high school poke fun at those with mental handicaps. The jokes they played on these individuals were cruel and thoughtless. I was shocked that many supposedly good citizens joined in this horseplay. In a sense, they were following the mob just as much as those who rode with the KKK did. At my high school, no one was being killed, but nevertheless people were being injured.

We are all surrounded by opportunities to get into situations where we can hurt others by our actions or, if we say nothing, by our inaction. The best way to avoid having to say "I'm sorry" is to think before you speak. If you think about the ramifications of your words or actions, you will walk away from the mob or become the voice of reason that stops the mob before it can act. So always allow your principles to shape your words. Don't get caught up in the fever.

The Courage to Speak Up

1. Don't talk about people behind their back. It reflects badly on you, causing you to lose influence in your world. Don't participate in any group that compromises your principles. Many politicians have "sold their souls" for votes only to have it come back to haunt them. Remember, your words and deeds will follow you.

2. When you fail to act or say something while others run someone down, you are as guilty as they are. In politics, it has become common practice to distort an opponent's record and personal life. This has in turn influenced the way we make fun of others. But those who stoop to this practice will find

that their words have little or no impact. Likewise, if you fail to stand up for someone, you will lose your impact with that person.

3. Realize what would happen if just one person stood up and said, "This is wrong." A young college student stood up against Nazi Germany during World War II. Sophie Scholl, along with her brother and some friends, distributed papers outlining the sins of the German government under Hitler. When it was discovered that Sophie was one of those behind "The White Rose" papers, she paid for her stand with her life. Yet her words did not die. In fact, the words she was executed for helping to write—the truth about Hitler and his government—were later reprinted and dropped over Germany by Allied bombers. Sophie's leaflets inspired thousands to join the underground to resist the Nazi madness. So be one of those who stands on principle and doesn't shrink back in the face of the mob mentality. If someone is being unfairly attacked or if lies are being told, then set the record straight. Don't worry about the cost; you will gain self-respect and a clear conscience.

For thirty years, Jim Wright served Texas as a representative to the United States Congress. In many of his sixteen campaigns, he ran against the same individual. Even though they disagreed on many issues, they never sank to name-calling or personal attacks. Because of this, many years later, when his opponent died, it was Jim Wright who was called upon to speak at the man's funeral. Being respectful and carefully choosing your words means that you won't be faced with embarrassment.

A Final Thought

For your words to have impact, they must be backed up by actions. If you are going to say "I'm sorry; I was wrong," then you have to walk the walk that goes with that talk. If you don't, then nothing else you ever say will make an impact. If you won't stand up for others when they are being persecuted, then don't expect anyone to stand up for you.

My grandfather always said, "Don't say anything behind someone's back you wouldn't say to their face, and don't do anything to anyone you wouldn't allow them to do to you." If you live by this philosophy, and think before you speak, you will have little need to worry about finding the courage to say "I'm sorry." But when you do mess up, begin with an apology, and pave the way to make an impact on others around you.

11

Should We Be
So Forward

One thing that has done a great deal to save the written word is the internet. Email has provided a new medium for writing down our thoughts and experiences and sharing them with others.

When it first appeared, email was one of the most exciting things to happen in our culture in a while. Millions of people jumped online and reconnected with people they hadn't touched base with in years. But in short order the personal touch of the internet was all but lost not only in a sea of spam but in the hundreds of unwanted forwarded messages that people began to send to everyone in their address book. Even as prices for connections came down and the speed went up, the onslaught of spam and forwards drove many away from email and even off the web. But used properly, email presents one of the most wonderful opportunities each of us will ever have to positively impact the world. To make your emails count, you have to think before you hit the send button.

When I first went online more than a decade ago, I spent most of my time on the internet catching up with friends and family via email. In a matter of weeks, I had connected with scores of people I had not seen or heard from in years.

Reconnecting with so many friends energized me in ways I couldn't fully comprehend. I loved sharing information daily with these old friends who were now new email buddies. The words I received in these emails fueled a new passion and vigor in my life. I found myself swimming in vibrant ideas and embracing a host of fresh ways to look at the world. Most of all, I found I was valuing relationships more deeply than ever.

Yet within a few short years, things dramatically changed. As the novelty of email wore off, I found I was receiving more and more junk email and less and less of the personal email that meant so much to me. The large number of messages I received from my friends each day gradually slowed until eventually I was receiving just occasional notes. Soon I was using my email account principally for business.

What happened?

Email's Lost Appeal

Part of email's loss of appeal as a method of visiting with friends and family can be traced to cheaper long-distance phone rates and free cellular minutes. When the internet took off, cellular service was expensive and pretty much used only for business or by the wealthy. As it became cheaper and easier to stay in touch by phone from almost anywhere on the planet, email became less popular.

But I think a greater reason for email's declining appeal is simple misuse. Most of us simply don't think before we fire off our email messages. We don't stop to consider how our words might be taken, and we often don't proofread them for errors.

I have upset several people with email messages. I didn't mean to, but I simply hit send before I thought or proofread. All too often, what I meant to say was not what the person read. What caused the misunderstanding? Usually it was my leaving out a word or making a funny or sarcastic comment that came across the wrong way on the other end.

In one case, an actor I knew had given me behind-the-scenes information on some films that dramatically increased my appreciation of them when I watched them. So I sent him an email in which I thought I was addressing this fact while praising the magic of his work. When I received no reply, and then several other emails to him went unanswered, I became worried. I called him and discovered the actor had read my email as an insult. When I reread my message, I could understand why. He didn't know me well enough to under-stand my sense of humor and personality. Without meaning to, I had lost the trust of someone I had really started to care about. What was supposed to be positive, humorous praise turned out to be the recipe for disaster.

In other cases, I had dashed off quick email responses and without proofing them for typos. Once, I accidentally expressed approval for a project I detested because I left out the word *not*. As a result, several close friends and business associates got mad at me because they were told I endorsed something I had once told them I was against. One misplaced word made me appear to be two-faced.

Because it's quick and easy to use, email can be both a wonder and a terror. You have to use it carefully. Like a loaded gun, it can accidentally go off, hurting you and those you care about.

Making the Most of Email

1. Consider who is going to receive your email message. If they don't know you well, make sure you write in a straightforward way. Don't expect them to know you well enough to read between the lines. Spell out each of your thoughts carefully.

2. Proofread your work several times before you hit send. You can make a great point only to have it completely undone because you left out or added a single word. Once a statement that means the opposite of how you really feel gets online, it's almost impossible to take back. So proof, proof, and proof again.

3. Tell your story in a short, easy-to-read fashion. History shows us that the best-remembered speeches were concise and to the point. Lincoln's

"Gettysburg Address" is still quoted a century and a half later, and it was only a few minutes long. One of Christ's parables would take up just a few inches in an email. On the other hand, those who spoke for hours usually made no impact at all. Think of a way to convey your information using a very short space. You will then have a much better chance of making a deep impression.

4. Use the same rules for composition that you learned in school. Shortcuts, like not using capitals or proper punctuation, really don't save time, and they make it look as if you don't care enough about the person you are writing to lift your language to their level. If you care about the way you present your copy, it will stand a much better chance of being taken seriously and make you look much brighter.

5. Don't use abbreviations when corresponding with people you don't know well. BTW or ROFL might be easy for you to understand, but they still mean nothing to the majority of the population. A good rule to follow is that if it's not in the dictionary, stay away from it.

6. Use a spell-checker. In the past, it was easier to overlook bad spelling because spell-checkers weren't as common. Today, every email program has one, so misspelling words makes a writer ap-

pear to be lazy. A lazy writer rarely has the attention of others and makes little positive impact.

7. Care about what you are writing. If you feel strongly about the words you put on the screen, that will come across to the person reading your email. Your passion and the fact you are sharing that passion with them will indicate to them that you care.

8. Answer all private emails. Don't assume that just reading a message is enough. Someone cared enough to send you an email; at least take a few seconds to tell them you received it. You may love getting emails from people, but if you don't answer them, they will quit writing. Lack of response has driven many people off the net. They simply feel as if no one cared about what they were saying.

Impact beyond Friends and Family

Today's internet really can connect you with the world. In an instant, you can communicate your thoughts to newspapers, magazines, politicians, pundits, teachers, and preachers. This network allows your thoughts to be "heard." Legislation has been changed thanks to email. Television series have been saved because of email. Views have been heard because of email. But to make a real impact, you need to follow the same rules as you would sending email to friends. Be brief, direct, honest, and careful. Proofread what you write. Realize before you hit the send button that your email message will lock you into a position.

Many have declared that email campaigns might well become the strongest forms of lobbying in Washington, D.C. Much like the letters that flooded the Senate chambers in the movie *Mr. Smith Goes to Washington*, email letters can make an impact on the votes of Congress. Carefully chosen words can actually change the course of the nation. They can shape the world!

Email also has become the new medium for fan mail. Many entertainers have websites and encourage people to drop them an email. Some, like the Oak Ridge Boys, even carry on regular and individual online correspondence with their fans. And many stars gear their communication to keep fans abreast of the latest news regarding their careers.

Moreso than typical fan exchanges, email has allowed a host of fans to become friends of stars whom they never would have met in the past, even making an impact on the product that an entertainer is putting out. Because of email, ordinary people are affecting what is heard on radio and appears on TV and in theaters. That's real power that didn't exist until the internet.

Frustrated with Email

While email can be a very positive thing, many users find themselves wearied by it. Not only are they frustrated with commercial spam but users are also being buried under the litter of email forwarded by regular people. If you are one of the online litterbugs, many of your most important words are probably being lost in cyberspace.

I was taught as a child that you should never be too forward. At that time, being forward meant being pushy. Forwards today are known as email messages or attachments that recipients like so much they immediately send them on to others. I guess you could say that the term still does mean being pushy.

The biggest problem with forwarded emails is that they are generally ignored. I simply don't have the time or energy to wade through all of the forwards I'm sent. Most forwarded emails I receive go into the trash without my even reading them. And it's a shame that so many people now think of forwards as electronic junk mail, because there's still a lot of really good uplifting and informative messages roaming the net. They just get lost in the trash spread by unthinking or uncaring web users.

At their best, forwards allow us to share inspired moments, genuinely touching stories, and personal thoughts or photos. Sadly, so many people send forwarded messages that a friend of mine says it's like "taking hundreds of newspapers and dumping them in someone's front yard. There may be some good stories there, but in all the volume, you'll never find them. So all that is left to do is haul the papers to the trash bin."

This doesn't have to be the case. If something happens to you or you find a story that you feel a need to share, you can still have an impact, but only if you forward it wisely. If you forward everything to everyone, it's likely that little, if anything, you send will be read. If you forward just a couple of things each day to your friends, eventually they will quit reading a majority of them, and your ability to impact others with this powerful tool will be lost.

I have a friend on the West Coast who knows how much I love animals. When Kelli finds a story she thinks I need to read, she forwards it to me. She might forward anything from a cute dog photo to a story about legislation that needs to be addressed by our elected officials. I'm sure Kelli forwards other friends messages concerning her other areas of interest, but she doesn't send those to me. She knows what we have in common and sticks to that. As a result, I read every forwarded message Kelli sends my way. She is not alone; I know several other people who think about what others would enjoy before forwarding them a message. So I always read theirs as well. It doesn't take long to separate the wheat from the chaff when it comes to forwarded email.

Before You Forward

You should consider a few basic rules that will enable you to use forwarded emails as a powerful force. These commonsense rules really aren't different from what you would use when speaking to any person face to face.

1. Think before you send. Is this something you really need to share?

2. Recognize who the audience is. You write different things to different people, so do the same thing with forwards. Don't be lazy and just write one email for everyone. If a person doesn't have a dog, don't send them a warning about dog food.

3. Check and recheck your forwards. Make sure they are factual. This morning I got a forward that was supposedly composed by *60 Minutes'* Andy Rooney. A few minutes later, the sender sent me a correction saying that the forward was a fake, that Rooney didn't agree with most of it and wrote none of it. Needless to say, the sender was more than a bit embarrassed. Worst of all, people are still crediting what was written to Mr. Rooney.

4. Don't send out forwards just to send them out. Use forwards rarely. Remember, less is more. If you send out only things that really are special and then handpick your recipients (rather than just loading your entire address book), you will stand a much better chance of having what so touched you also deeply touch others.

5. Most important, follow one of my grandfather's rules for family gatherings—stay away from politics. Unless you know how a person stands, a simple forward stating a certain position or making fun of a certain politician might burn a bridge that can never be rebuilt. Limit the political forwards to political groups.

6. Always personalize the forward. If you want it to make an impact, tell those you are sending that forward to why you feel it's important for them to see it. Don't just hit a button and send it on!

7. If you can't say something nice, don't say anything at all, or in this case keep your hand off the forward button.

8. Forwarding information such as recipes, consumer updates, and other alerts can be good if you can answer yes to these two questions: Does this apply to the person who is receiving it? Is the information accurate? Many times I have gotten forwards from people with a consumer alert only to have that same person email me later to tell me the alert had been a hoax. On a couple of occasions, I have had to send out emails saying the same thing because I had already forwarded the forward. There is enough misinformation on the internet without our adding more. So be careful and do your research.

Personal Experiences Make the Most Impact

In the spring of 2007, a high school friend of mine died at the age of fifty-four. Janie's life had greatly impacted mine. Because her funeral was more than six hundred miles away, I was unable to attend. Yet thanks to the internet, I was able to sign the online guest book at the funeral home. I was also able to view what others had written there. As I read the online tribute page, I recognized that Janie's life could be an inspiration to a few of my friends who had never met her. Though I rarely forward anything, I carefully picked out a small number of email contacts and sent them an edited version of what I wrote on the online tribute page. This is what I forwarded:

A friend of mine from high school died this week. Her funeral is on Saturday in Missouri. Janie was a remarkable person and I wish each of you could have known her. She had juvenile diabetes, but it never held her back. She got married, had a child, and was a super mother, wife, and friend. When the disease took her eyesight, her husband could not handle it. He not only left her but got the courts to give him custody of their son. Still, Janie did not give up. She moved to St. Louis, went to the school for the blind, and rebuilt her life. While holding a job, she also returned to college, earning an education degree and finishing in the top 10 percent of her class. She even fell in love and married. This happened all after her blindness and after she had turned forty. Yet the disease didn't stop by taking her vision; it took her kidneys next. A transplant gave her some time, but by then her heart began to fail. Her husband, who also had diabetes, passed away two years ago. Yet this beautiful woman still continued to push on with life and stayed active in church and work, always led by her guide dog, Garbo. Janie's huge heart finally gave out this week. The following is what I wrote on her tribute page at the funeral home.

I knew Jane as Janie. My life with her revolved around high school experiences that were far too few. As I look back through more than thirty-five years, the images of most of those I knew during that time are hazy and undefined. Yet when my mind locks onto Janie, I can so clearly see her smiling face and bright eyes that it is as if she were standing in front of me right now. And I can hear her too. Her voice was like a simple, uplifting melody that hung in the air long after she had disappeared. She was such a breath of fresh air that I still smile every time I think of her.

My memories of Janie are so sharply imprinted because my impressions of her were not only noted by my mind, they were felt in my heart. She was so sweet, and not the kind of surface sweetness that always rings hollow; rather hers was the sincere sweetness that poured from a person who cared deeply about others. And my, how the love freely poured from her heart.

To this day I believe that Janie was the most beautiful girl in our high school class. In my mind there is no doubt. Yet the essence of how beautiful she really was presented itself in the way she battled the demons that tried so hard to wreck her delicate life. She never gave up and never quit smiling. In high school I had no idea of the insidious nature of the disease that ultimately took her from this world far too soon. I wish I had known it then, because I would have fully understood and appreciated her courage, determination, and faith. But Janie didn't show the pain, reveal the mountains that she had to climb each day, or unveil the illness that haunted her each night. She was simply too busy living — chasing the next dream or looking for the next ray of sunshine — to worry about the heavy price that came with each new breath. Thus none of us realized what a fragile being she was.

On December 31, 1970, I was blessed to welcome the New Year in with Janie. At midnight her smile — that whimsical, slightly bent, one-of-a-kind smile — lit up the room like a searchlight. I didn't realize it then, but that moment reflected what Janie was always to be. She was and remains a beacon, a bright, shining gift from God that blessed us in such incredible ways that her image, personality, faith, and determination remain in sharp focus. Thank you, Janie, for touching our lives and leaving us so much richer for the experience. The world is a better place because you were here, and we are better for having you in our lives.

Just like Janie made an impression in my life, the email made an impression on others. I later found out that sharing her story with a carefully selected group brought forth some special reactions. Many people, realizing the fragility of life, called up some of their old friends and shared memories with them. Others gave funds to a guide-dog group. A few opted to pass on to others what I had written. In time the forward took on a life of its own. I even discovered that Janie's story had found its way into the hands of thousands of pastors and had been used in some of their messages and reprinted in their newsletters.

I believe that the reason my forward on Janie's life had a chance to make an impact was that I rarely forward anything. Thus, those who received it sensed its importance. If I had been sending out a dozen forwards every day to everyone in my address book, Janie's story probably would have been immediately trashed.

My forward, sent to only a handful of my friends, managed to touch a few thousand people. It expanded the impact of Janie's courage and wisdom. While this example provides just a snapshot of the power of the internet when you carefully choose an audience for your words, the following true life story takes that power to a whole other level.

The Real Power of Forwards

Long before the advent of the internet and email, Helga Schmidt was doing a bit of Christmas shopping at a small department store in a rural Kansas community. After picking out several items, she got in line at the business's one cash register. In front of Helga were two small and very excited children holding a box containing a single pair of women's slippers. As the clerk rang up the purchase, the children discovered they were almost three dollars short. Though she was in a hurry to get home for supper, Helga nevertheless asked the little boy who the slippers were for and why it was so important to have this specific pair. The child shared a story that so deeply touched the woman, she paid for the shoes.

Helga Schmidt's story of the gift shoes would have ended there if she hadn't shared it with a continuing education class she taught. Moved by the story of a son and a daughter who wanted to buy a pair of slippers for their dying mother, her students also passed that story on to their friends and family. Over the course of the next two decades, the tale was even placed on the back of a few church bulletins in the Midwest and found its way into one of the *Chicken Soup* books. In twenty years, a great many people were enriched by this story of giving and love.

In the mid-1990s, someone whose name we don't know took the story of the shoes and transposed it into a text file that they attached to an email. Little did they realize that within months that email would find its way to points all over the globe. Thanks to the internet, countless numbers of people received and read the story.

Eddie Carswell, a member of the award-winning singing group Newsong, was one of those who discovered the story of the slippers in his email in-box. Carswell was moved to turn the real-life experience into a song. That song, "The Christmas Shoes," would become the first Christmas hit of the twenty-first century. Its powerful imagery and moving music made such a huge impact on the American public that the story was transformed into a bestselling book and a highly acclaimed CBS movie.

When she shared the story of "The Christmas Shoes" for the very first time, Helga Schmidt never intended the small bit of Americana she witnessed to spawn a hit song, a movie, and a book. She figured the story would quickly fade from everyone's mind but her own. Yet thanks to the internet, the actions of those two children who simply told a stranger, "We want to give these special slippers to our mother so that she will have something to wear when she walks the golden streets in heaven," brought millions to tears and reemphasized the meaning of love, hope, and faith. That is how much impact one carefully written and sent email can have.

12

Endless Possibilities

The New World of the Web and Texting

In 2005 a carefree sixteen-year-old student in Michigan was meandering through his life unconcerned about his future. He was simply living day by day, moment to moment. With a quick smile and jovial nature, Miles Levin was often the center of his universe, the boy whom others followed.

Then Miles was sideswiped by alveolar rhabdomyosarcoma, a relentless cancer that pushes through a body slowly, painfully strangling muscle tissue. In the time it took for a doctor to make his diagnosis and explain the disease, Miles went from a boy with a boundless future to one struggling to live a day at a time.

In many ways, Miles was just like a million other cancer patients across the globe. He was all but unknown, fighting a disease that strikes not just the body but the spirit and mind as well. One of the sad facts about cancer is that it often scares away friends, making those who struggle to challenge the disease solitary soldiers on the battlefield of uncertainty. As the shock of the news hit his friends, it seemed that Miles would be fighting a lonely war, confined to his small world and perhaps doomed to die almost anonymously.

While being treated through long rounds of chemotherapy, Miles discovered that Beaumont Hospital in Royal Oak, Michigan, had a place where patients could express their hopes and fears in their own words. Inspired, Miles started writing. His blog entries were put on the hospital's website, and family and friends could easily connect with him and get a better sense of what he was going through each day.

Miles was picking up on something that first evolved from websites. In the early days of the internet, many informational websites had buttons for "latest news." Many of these sections were updated so often that they were called "log entries." In a few menus these were called "weblogs." Sensing a way to set those who posted running commentaries in these logs apart from regular news updates, a regular "web logger" named Peter Merholz coined the term "blog." Soon, blogs evolved from regular news updates to become expressions of personal opinions or experiences.

Better than most, Miles sensed that a blog could educate and bring hope. Maybe because of his youth, he saw the medium's potential and understood that it could unite others who were also locked in solitary life-and-death battles. Rather than just quickly putting a few random thoughts in his blog, he wrote from the heart, bringing wit and youthful enthusiasm to a very dark world. Within months, his blog audience had grown to thousands.

While others struggled to find answers as to why, often blaming God for their problems, Miles laughed at his pain, suffering, and illness by writing, "It's always something." He then turned his words to explain how six straight days of nausea had been followed by a sweet afternoon of beautiful sunshine. He shared that experiencing the one wonderful day made going through a week's misery seem not so bad.

Miles found his voice in his blog, describing trials and emotions that others could grasp only through his words. His later writings showed he understood the power he had found on the web: "Unlike many cancer patients, I don't have much anger. The way I see it, we're not entitled to one breath of air. We did nothing to earn it, so whatever we get is a bonus. I might be more than a little disappointed with the hand I've been dealt, but this is what it is. Thinking about what it could be is pointless. It ought to be different, that's for sure, but it ain't. A moment spent moping is a moment wasted.

"I accept what is to come, but I cannot rid myself of a deep mourning for all those experiences — college, marriage, children, grandchildren — that will probably never be mine to celebrate. What solace I do find is in the knowledge that I have done everything I can to transmute this terribleness into something positive by showing as many people as I can how to endure it with a smile."

Though he never planned it, Miles had become a celebrity. People from all over the world began to email him, seeking his advice on everything from the fragility of life to how to find joy in the moment.

As with many cancer patients, Miles's ride was filled with mountains and valleys. Hope was almost always followed by despair, promises were given and taken away every day, and the cancer would come and go as if taunting him. Yet through it all he continued to write, reshaping his goals and refining his ability to describe his emotions. And always at the heart of every word he placed on his blog was his honesty. At one point, as he sensed the end was near, he wrote that perhaps he had been put on earth to show people how to die with grace.

Ultimately, Miles came to understand the gift he had been given through his struggle. Thanks to his blog, he was touching more lives than most people do in a hundred years of living. In the weeks before he died, he compared his life to a golfer swinging at a bucket of golf balls. "Now with just a handful left, each swing becomes more meaningful," he wrote.

Miles lived to graduate from high school but passed away before he could fulfill his dream of attending college. Yet even cheated out of so much, he never grew bitter. And online, readers still find great hope in some of his final words: "I am living more richly than I ever was before cancer. Dying is not what scares me; it's dying having had no impact. I know a lot of eyes are watching me suffer, and—win or lose—this is my time for impact."

Making Your Mark with a Modern Tool

Miles Levin understood the power of the web and how to use it in a positive way. The web allowed his words to have tremendous impact and his life to have greater meaning than he ever could have hoped just a decade before. In fact, without the web, Miles probably would have died without being able to spell out the great lessons he learned. Certainly, without his blog, he wouldn't have inspired thousands of others to face their most trying days with the same courage and joy as he did. Without the web, his story never would have been felt beyond his family and friends.

While no one wants to go through what Miles experienced, most of us would like to follow his lead and make a lasting and meaningful impact on the world. With the internet, that has become much easier than ever before. The problem is putting out a meaningful message that doesn't get buried by the huge amount of trash online.

Today, services like MySpace, Facebook, and online personal blogs, such as Miles used, have tried to replicate journals and diaries. But while they do shed a great deal of light on those who pen them, and they probably do an effective job of recording certain memories for sharper mental playback later, because these entries are always in the public eye, they are often less personal and often far less honest than the old fashioned way of "writing it down."

When I review the many blogs that are out there, I find that Miles's blog is the exception to the rule. Many blogs seem to jump into either an attack mode or serve as forums to express editorial opinions or rants. Much like talk radio, they have evolved into something many perceive as negative.

To make a real impact, you have to do what Miles did; be honest and sincere and provide information that is unique and needed. The first part of the equation should be easy, but the last part is very tough.

Like Miles, Roger Bennett was hit by cancer. Roger, an award-winning gospel music songwriter and pianist, had a fan base that allowed him a large and immediate forum to express his feelings about his battle with the disease. Armed with a well-established website, Roger spent more than two years writing of his victories and losses, his hopes and dreams, and his fears and faith. His words were almost addictive. In the face of what seemed to be a sure path to death, he was able to provide light for all who read his commentaries. Like Miles, his joy in spending time engaged in the little pleasures of life, like watching the changing seasons or eating a bowl of ice cream, provided stark lessons of blessings that most of those who were reading his blogs had forgotten. When he died, Roger's influence was greater than it had ever been as an entertainer. More than even on the stage and in the spotlight, on the internet he had provided the inspiration others needed to fully live each moment of their lives.

A New Way to Create a Community

A blog allows you to create a new online group of friends. A blog gives you the chance to invite others into your life and share insight into the things you treasure as well as provide your expertise and opinions.

There are almost thirty million blogs in the world, and that number is growing every day. A large percentage of these are created by common folks who want to find a way to share something from their lives.

One of my hobbies is car restoration, so I read a few blogs on this subject. I'm constantly learning new tips on everything from types of oil to use in vintage vehicles to the best ways to prepare a car for a show.

My wife is an educator. She reads blogs on subjects like reading recovery. She finds that the experiences of teachers in the classroom help her learn new methods to reach kids who are struggling to learn.

In the past, most of us could rely only on the advice of those we knew. But thanks to blogs, we can tap into the minds of those who aren't in the same place we are, reading about ideas and methods we never would have been privy to a generation ago. Thanks to how easy it is to blog, you can get up and running in no time. And your words can make an impact beyond what you can even begin to imagine.

You don't have to be hit by a traumatic disease to use your words for positive purposes in a blog. There's a need for bloggers in every possible area. Teachers, doctors, nurses, and even teens—just about anyone can offer advice and provide positive information that others are seeking. And while it might be tempting to gain an audience by going negative and attacking others or their causes, you have a much better chance of making a long-term impact by seeking ways to provide comfort, experience, education, or expertise.

I read blogs on everything from animal care to motion pictures to health issues. I use blogs that answer questions about my hobbies or help me find information on subjects that interest me. My college son even writes blogs to interest kids his age in discovering classic films. Most of the blogs I read are great, but I don't think I am cut out to write my own, at least not yet.

Are You Cut Out to Be a Blogger?

1. Do you have insight or expertise on a unique subject? Successful blogs are specialized. They focus on one thing.
2. Do you have the desire and self-discipline to keep your blog up? Blog audiences expect to see new material on a regular schedule.
3. Do you feel comfortable putting yourself and your ideas on display? In many ways, you will be walking into the cyberworld naked.

1. Can you take criticism? You will probably receive some negative responses or sincere questions that might not be easy to take or to answer.

5. Can you sustain a blog? For Miles and Roger, the disease they fought constantly gave them new perspectives on life, and so they never ran out of material. Someone working overseas in the third world might have an endless supply of stories that folks back home would find fascinating. But how deep is your well?

6. Do you have energy, time, and creativity? A blog that makes a real impact is almost always created by someone who sees the world a bit differently, has a few hours each week to put that vision into a written form, and has the fuel to keep the mental engine going. The University of Oklahoma's Sheri Coale often blogs on her experiences as a college women's basketball coach. Sheri is bright and articulate and has a knack for seeing a life lesson in almost everything she does. She also is not afraid to spotlight the way she messes up. Her blog is incredibly popular and probably is instrumental in providing her program with a very positive impact.

7. Good blogging is always honest. Whether you're creating a blog that tells the story of your fight with a disease or is focused on the joys of owning a cat, what you write has to be honest. Readers see through people who aren't being straight with

them. Honesty often means revealing shortcomings or mistakes to others. Not everyone can do that, but those who can be open are well on their way to reaching out and touching others in a positive way.

I saved honesty until last for a reason. Most people simply can't fully embrace honesty. Miles and Roger did. They weren't afraid to admit their weaknesses and doubts. These days we constantly hear about natural resources that are in short supply. Well, it seems that honesty is leading that list. It's hard to find folks who embrace what Harry Truman called "plain speaking." In fact, there seems to be a real lack of honesty on most blogs.

Perhaps that's because honesty comes at a cost. For example, losing children to death, losing a limb or one's sight, or making what you consider to be an unpardonable mistake are all difficult enough experiences to go through once, but blogging about them forces you to relive those experiences. This is tough, but your willingness to be honest might well be the key that helps others avoid that pain or at least gives them the strength to go through the ordeal.

Blogging can take your experiences and wisdom to the world and give you great satisfaction while providing others with joy, comfort, or understanding. Keeping a blog going is a challenge, and it's not for everyone, but never before in the history of humankind have individuals had more opportunity to make a statement and have it heard.

Changing the World One Life at a Time

Blogging is a relatively new tool, and yet in a brief period of time, it has been used to save millions of lives. People who have read blogs have identified illnesses at the earliest time and found ways to treat them before they became life threatening. Blogs have helped in the classroom, in hospitals, in churches, and in every imaginable hobby.

In 2006 Larissa, a twenty-one-year-old American college student, became interested in the plight of the many children in Africa who have been orphaned by AIDS. Through her church, Larissa was introduced to this subject through a blog written by a Kenyan woman who had started an orphanage and school in Nairobi. Reading this woman's online diary brought the great needs in this part of the world to life. Consumed by a desire to help, Larissa began to save money to make a trip to Kenya. In early 2007, she visited the home.

Within a week of her arrival in Africa, Larissa knew she had found her calling. Filled with passion, she began to write a blog titled Karma House. In it she shared the story of her work and addressed the specific needs of the children she met. Readers of Larissa's blog were touched, and soon many gave gifts to address those needs. Thanks to her sharing what she saw, many children's lives were enhanced.

Larissa's trip to Africa was only three months long, but during that time she found a need that wasn't being met.

Back in the States, she shared through her blog the plight of high school graduates who had the intelligence but not the money to attend college. Largely thanks to Karma House, several young women found sponsors, and Larissa is now looking at buying a home for them. She has even moved to Kenya, is involved in helping "her" girls, and is still writing her blog. This young woman is one of millions who is living her dream thanks to sharing her heart and passion online.

Bringing People Together or Bringing People Down?

Recent studies have found that while individuals come in contact with many more people than in the past, the twenty-first century is a time when people feel more lonely and isolated than ever before. It's hard to believe, but hundreds of thousands in New York City cannot point to anyone they are close to. Essentially, they work and shop in the bustling urban world, but they have removed themselves from any meaningful human contact. They are as alone as if they lived on a mountaintop.

For many, their only source of human contact is internet message boards.

A message board is a group of people who share a common interest. Many are social clubs for friendship or dating. Others center on people's interest in sports, arts, or entertainment. Thousands bring people together to share information on politics, medicine, and even hobbies.

They are essentially forums for people to state their opinions or questions online in the hope of connecting with someone who will react to their words.

Sadly, many of these boards bring out the worst in people. They embrace subject matter that is depraved and in some cases illegal. While these boards seem to be everywhere, there are also many boards that unite people in ways that have the potential to be positive and uplifting. The biggest problem with even a majority of these boards is not with their goals but with those who post. Most posters have user names, allowing them to hide behind secret identities and act in ways they never would in public. All too often this leads to posts that do more harm than good. It seems that what message boards lack is a cyber version of Emily Post.

Message Board Etiquette

1. Write your posts as if you were speaking to a person face to face. Write nothing on the board that you wouldn't say in public. You would be surprised at the number of people who ordinarily don't use foul language who seem to enjoy swearing online.

2. No matter the type of board, take the high road. If you want to make a positive impact, don't be combative; instead, write posts that reflect your thinking without attacking others.

3. Show respect. Treat others on the board as if they lived next door to you. On message boards, it's really easy to get baited into shouting matches

that often sink to the level of personal attacks.
Most of us would never allow this to happen in real
life. It's best to follow Teddy Roosevelt's example
of speaking softly (or in this case writing politely)
and carrying a big stick (providing information that
supports your point of view).

4. Be yourself. Don't develop an alter ego that you
   would be ashamed for others to see in public. If
   you treat the message boards just as you do conversations with friends, your words will have much
   more weight than those of people who employ
   inflammatory methods to make their points.

5. Post only things that you know are true. Don't fill
   cyberspace with rumors or half-truths. Just as in
   real life, when you are found out, your words will
   have little impact.

6. Stay away from any board that constantly makes
   you angry. We rarely say anything of substance
   when enraged. So if you find yourself in a board
   that has become little more than a forum for
   verbal abuse, divorce yourself from it and find a
   community that reflects your values. You will be
   much happier and have a better chance to make a
   point that hits home.

A Matter of Trust

Message boards essentially are communities. Some are
very small and there is little traffic; others are as heavily

populated and congested as New York City. But whatever the size and purpose of the board, forming relationships online isn't much different than in any other community.

Two people who lived more than a thousand miles apart were using a chat room in the summer of 2007 when one of them shared some medical issues she had been having. The other party recognized her symptoms and suggested she seek immediate medical attention. Because she had come to trust his words during other conversations on the message board, the woman dropped everything and went to an emergency room, where she was treated for a stroke. Doctors later told her that if she had waited even a few more hours, she would have suffered a more serious stroke and probably would have died.

This is just one of many stories illustrating how solid information shared on message boards or in chat rooms has the power to save lives. Yet consider the alternative. More than a century ago, Mark Twain wrote, "A lie can circle the earth before truth gets its boots on." One of the sad truths of the information age is that lies now travel at cyberspeed. If the man whose advice saved the woman had been the sort of person who often used attacks and lies to establish his place on the message board, the woman probably would have ignored his vital advice and might have died as an indirect result of his online methodology. So be as careful in how you conduct yourself with your message board buddies as you would with the friends in your physical community. After all, someone's life might depend on their trusting you.

Should You Start a Message Board?

Running a message board can be very rewarding and can offer a way for many in a cybercommunity to make a real impact with their thoughts and words. But there are drawbacks. Ask yourself some important questions before you take on the responsibility of running a board.

1. Do you have enough knowledge about the board's subject matter to be a good moderator? If you know nothing about cats and you decide to run a cat-care board, you are in way over your head right from the beginning. You have to know enough to make sure good information is being posted on the board.

2. Do you have the time it takes to police a board? Being a cop is often hard work. Boards are constantly being attacked by individuals and even companies with divisive goals. And because your board is a reflection on you, you have to constantly check to make sure your board represents your own morality.

3. Will you still be motivated to run the board a year later? A board is a community. How would you feel if you moved into a community, enjoyed the people you met there, then found yourself evicted

and out of touch with everyone else in town? This happens whenever a board is shut down.

Message Boards Can Be a Great Tool

Several years ago, a family member discovered they had a rare type of cancer. The first thing I did was hop online for a Google search to find a group that discussed this illness. After I read several posts, what seemed to be a hopeless situation suddenly seemed manageable. I learned about effective new treatments and conversed with several people who had beaten that type of cancer. On this site I found the names of doctors and hospitals that special-ize in new treatments, and board posters even provided encouraging words and prayers. In a matter of minutes after receiving my family member's bad news, I was part of a community that pitched in with great support and knowledge.

While the most popular boards on the web often seem to be only about stirring things up and providing a forum for angry people to discuss politics, religion, or sports, there are lots of "quiet places" out there where people are making wonderful relationships. In that kind of forum, you can change lives for the better with your carefully written advice.

What about Chatting?

Chat rooms are message boards on speed. They are instant. Your words appear as quickly as the words you speak on a phone. To have the greatest positive impact in this new arena, you must think before you react. In most cases, you are conversing with people you don't know, and an offhanded comment a friend would understand might be taken the wrong way.

Chat rooms can also be dangerous places, potentially leading to your being stalked or having personal information revealed on the internet. As an adult, those are risks we should be aware of and be careful to avoid. Children, though, can be more easily taken advantage of. Stalkers are ready to prey on youngsters with unsupervised access to chat rooms. So parents must guard this area of the net very closely. Just as we tell our kids not to speak with strange adults in public, we should teach them to apply that rule online as well. And if we do allow them to chat it up, we need to make sure they don't reveal personal information that can lead someone to them. Like talks about sex and drugs, this is one parent-to-child conversation that needs to happen early and be repeated often.

On the positive side, chatting can be a great way to stay updated in the important areas of your life. Just be sure to apply the same rules to your use of this communication tool as you would to forums, email, or phone conversations.

Texting

It's hot, it's out there, and it's replacing email as a great way to stay in touch. The rules here are simple.

1. Don't be wordy. Say what you want as quickly as you can.
2. Don't use it unnecessarily. You're not the only one footing the bill. When you send a message, the recipient pays too.
3. Don't do it while you're driving.
4. And remember, while it's quick, it doesn't have the impact of other forms of communication. So use it for quick updates, but not as a substitute for writing or calling.

Be Yourself!

Blogs and message boards, as well as their cousins, the cybergroups and chat rooms, provide dynamic forums for voicing our opinions. Yet for our words to have lasting and positive impact, we must carefully consider our place in these new communities. If you want what you write to be taken seriously, be the same person online as you are off. And if you discover that you aren't the kind of person you would like to be in either place, then go back to chapter 1 of this book and start working on a new way of talking to yourself before you talk online.

13

Prayer and Praise

When a person has little chance of succeeding, people often say, "They haven't got a prayer." Though some might argue, I'd say that a person has fallen into a very sad state when others point out that he or she is "prayerless." If you are so isolated from the world that no one cares enough to send out a prayer for you, then you really *are* alone. If the odds against you are so long that people believe even the Almighty cannot come to your rescue, then you are in a very bad situation. I prefer to look at things another way; there's always hope, and there's always a prayer that can provide the reason for that hope.

In Our Prayers

Countless times, I've heard news anchors, government officials, and even close friends say, "We will keep you in our prayers." I often wonder how many people actually follow up on this pledge. I fear it's very few. More often than not this statement carries as little weight as saying, "Have a good day!"

This is all the more surprising in light of recent studies that reveal that prayer seems to help people recover from serious illnesses. In these studies, half of the people in the test group were not prayed for and the other half were prayed for by organized prayer teams. Neither group of patients knew who was being prayed for. In the various reports, the patients who had the fastest recoveries were those who had been singled out in prayer. Scientists were at a loss to "logically" explain the results, but it did lead them to admit that there must be something to asking for God's help.

In the winter of 2007, a close friend of mine was felled by not one but two brain aneurysms. For weeks she lingered on life support, growing weaker each day. As her condition deteriorated, her children were called in to say their goodbyes, and her church prepared for a funeral. Then Linda suddenly snapped out of her coma. As she came to, she looked over at her husband and asked, "Where is everybody else?"

Shaking his head, he explained, "They allow only one of us at a time in ICU. There is no one else here."

Linda argued, "No, I heard them. They were all speaking at the same time, and there were hundreds of them too. Some of them I knew; others I didn't. But they were all around me. They were here!"

Linda's husband assured her that all those people had never been in the room. Like many, he initially thought that Linda must have been hallucinating. Some people speculated that Linda had seen and heard angels. But the real answer was probably much closer to home.

A few days after her miraculous recovery, Linda discovered that a large prayer chain had been created to pray for her. This group had been formed when news of her condition was sent out to local churches, and then it had spread to other groups throughout the region. Within days Linda's name had been placed on hundreds of prayer lists and written in scores of prayer logs. For weeks, thousands were praying for her each day. Her miraculous recovery convinced Linda of two things: the voices she had heard were of the people who had been praying for her, and those prayers had pulled her back from death's door.

Linda's story is far from unusual. Countless people have been touched by the power of prayer. Science and personal experiences have proven that the words of prayer do have impact. But that impact can't happen unless the ones doing the praying believe their words carry weight.

Prayer with Impact

Despite stories like Linda's, many people will argue that prayer is simply a waste of time. Even many believers think God is too busy to listen to their special needs. Others think that because of their shortcomings or sins, they don't deserve to have God's ear. They feel unworthy to approach God in prayer. Yet studies also have proven that people who pray are healthier, happier, and experience less stress than those who don't. So there are a host of great reasons to believe that words spoken in prayer have the potential for great impact in your life as well as in the lives of those for whom you are praying. There are solid reasons to take the time each day to pray.

Reading some of the scores of wonderful books available on how to pray might help you to feel more power as you pray. But if you are just beginning to think about using prayer in your life, here are a few simple suggestions to put into immediate practice.

1. Be yourself. You don't have to sound like a preacher, you don't have to speak in King James English, and you don't have to use fifty-cent words. If you have ever watched the TV series *The Waltons*, consider how Grandpa Walton prayed. He showed great respect but spoke just as he would to a member of his family. God made you, and he knows you, so pray as you are.

2. Be direct and simply say what's on your heart. If you have a need, spell it out in a way that you would understand. If you are praying for someone else, mention their need specifically.

3. Don't demand answers. As the country song says, sometimes you need to thank God for unanswered prayers.

4. As in conversations with your friends, don't be selfish. Ask for what you really need, not what you want, and then pray for others who need much

more. Focus on others in every area of your life, and you will be a much happier person. This is true in prayer as well.

5. Make prayer a habit. Most of us, even those who claim to be nonbelievers, pray when the bullets are flying around us. As the proverb says, "There are no atheists in foxholes." Praying every day will keep your prayers on a higher plain and you will be able to keep track of the results. Actress and charity worker Catherine Hicks told me she prays while on her treadmill. I have a friend who prays while commuting in his car to work. I like to pray while jogging. There are no rules; you don't have to close your eyes or hit your knees, but being consistent in time and location helps most continue the practice day in and day out.

6. Let those you are praying for know that you are praying for them. Few resent having others praying for them, and it lifts the spirits of most just to know someone cares enough to send up a request on their behalf. I have a friend I rarely speak to or hear from, but on days when I pray for her, it seems she always emails me. I feel she is somehow being touched by what I am saying. When she contacts me and I explain I have just prayed for her, she is always amazed.

7. Even on days when it seems your prayer is not getting out of your room, continue to voice your

blessings and concerns until you are finished. As you see prayer work in your life, you will come to believe that even on your bad days, someone is hearing what you are praying.

8. Consider keeping a prayer log. A lot of people need to keep track of something to keep doing it. They need to record their results. I have many friends who jog who record the time of every workout and the distance they covered. For some, having a log allows them to see the results of their prayers. So if you are a detail-oriented person, this might work for you. On the other hand, if having to keep a log will discourage you from making prayer a habit, don't bother.

For most people, prayer works best if it's a habit. So find a way to fit it into your lifestyle, if only for a few minutes each day. If you do, your prayers will likely have much more impact.

Prayer Is Not the Only Tool

One of the most fascinating stories in the New Testament is when Christ used a few fish and a couple of loaves of bread to feed thousands. I am not a theologian, but I am drawn to one very human facet of this story. Christ fed people before he preached. What this says to me is that people listen a lot better when they're not hungry.

I recently spoke with a man whose business is providing compassion to some of the poorest people in the world. John Cathcart is a missionary and heads up a large organization that runs orphanages, distributes food, and drills wells in the third world. He was recently onsite when a drilling operation struck water in the middle of an African desert. One old man of the village, after observing the youngsters of his tribe playing in the fresh, clean water, approached John and asked a simple question: "Did your God do this?" That question opened the door to converting a large number of local people to the Christian faith. But without the work that preceded them, the words John shared with the old man would have had no impact.

In a world where so many people are hungry or in anguish, it's always best to find ways to meet those pressing needs before trying to offer your words of spiritual wisdom. Reach out to those around you rather than lecturing them on how to live their lives. If they see your faith in your actions, they will be much more open to hearing what you have to say. When they sense your genuine compassion, the soil has been prepared for your words to take root in.

Slam-Dunk Faith

In the mid-1950s, one of the finest young men ever to come out of Fort Worth, Texas, was involved in an auto accident. In one brief moment, Ron Ballard went from being a college basketball player to a person who would forever be confined either to a wheelchair or a bed. Paralyzed from the neck down, Ron faced a drastically restricted life. And if it weren't for the influence of one very special woman, that might have become the reality.

Elizabeth Swank had been Ron's Sunday school teacher when he was in high school. After the devastating accident, she made it a point to come to see the young man each week. During these visits, she caught him up on local events, filled him in on what his friends were doing, and even shared a bit of her weekly lessons. She also listened to him, showed respect for his ideas, and encouraged him not to give up. She assured him that even though he couldn't move from the neck down, he still could make an impact on those around him. No matter how he looked to others, she emphasized that in her eyes, he wasn't helpless and his voice still carried weight.

Swank's faithfulness and prayers continued not just for weeks or months but for years. Ultimately, Ron grew past feeling sorry for himself and began to believe that Mrs. Swank was right.

One day, the essence of what the woman had shared sparked an idea in Ron's mind. Five decades ago, there were no handicapped parking places, handicap-accessible buildings, or easy ways for those with major handicaps to travel. With his Sunday school teacher taking notes, he shared a concept for a barrier-free building where men and women with handicaps could worship. Swank did more than just praise the idea; she put feet to her words of encouragement. She first lived her faith by getting others to help her transport Ron to their church. Then together the teacher and student sold others on their idea. Together, they kept pushing it, and eventually the church raised money to make Ron's dream a reality. On a Sunday morning in the mid-1950s, Crusader's Chapel opened, with Ron greeting the first guest from his wheelchair.

Crusader's Chapel was an immediate success in two ways. Initially, it gave those with handicaps someplace to meet and feel whole. It was a place where their spirits could be fed. Even if that was all that came from this project, it would have been remarkable. Yet it was what Ron's idea accomplished in the long run that made the real impact. The chapel showed the leadership of the city of Fort Worth that by changing a few little things, they could open up their community to those with severe handicaps. Thus began a movement that led to ramps, larger doors, handicapped parking spaces, and a host of other revolutionary ideas that we now see in every community in the United States. None of this would have happened without Elizabeth Swank's faithfulness, prayers, and encouragement. She not only talked the talk but lived it each and every day. Through the support and prayers of one woman, an incredible movement was started that has impacted the lives of millions.

Creating Words of Inspiration

In addition to living the faith, we also need to encourage others who are living it. How often do we stop when we see individuals we admire and tell them how much they inspire us? By and large most faithful people who give their time and energy to help others rarely know how much they are appreciated. They need to hear it. By praising their efforts, we give them the fuel to continue to make an impact with their lives. Our words become a part of the work they are doing. And we also can use our words to help others who are struggling to find the faith they need to achieve something special. Ron Ballard had given up on life until his Sunday school teacher convinced him he was still capable of doing special things. All around us are people who see their limits rather than their potential. A part of faith is lifting others up so they can do great things.

I am constantly wowed by my sons' friends. So many of these young people have so much talent, energy, and enthusiasm. Yet one of the things I have found is that deep down most of these young people often lack the confidence to pursue their dreams. As they reach their last years of high school and begin college, most question whether they have what it takes to make it in the real world.

Not long ago, my wife and I were blown away by one of our youngest son's new friends. Lauren is a talented vocalist, smart, vivacious, and beautiful. Yet as I got to know her, I sensed a certain lack of self-confidence. What caused this bit of personal doubt? Only this: Lauren is short. At just four foot nine, she's a bit below what society sees as the norm. So here was this young woman who I felt could be stopped by nothing, who I believed had unlimited potential, and she seemed hesitant because of her height.

I wanted to tell Lauren that all of us imagine flaws where there are none. I can't begin to count the number of people who fail to voice their opinions, much less chase their dreams, because they think they are too short, tall, skinny, fat, slow, fast, dim or bright, too ugly or too handsome ... the list goes on. Many hold back because they are women or the wrong color or think they were simply born at the wrong time. The fact is that each of us has potential and none of us is perfect. Yet telling someone that they need to ignore their imagined limitations is almost as bad as agreeing with their biggest fear that they won't succeed. So what do you do? The best place to start is to find a role model for those who need a bit of a helping hand.

We are all made in God's image, so we have a pretty good starting point for success. We were also all put on earth for a reason, so we are anything but worthless. We also all change the world by simply being here. Note that I didn't say we have the potential to change the world. No, we all *change* the world! The question is whether we are going to change it in a positive or a negative way. And how we talk to others, the way we show our faith to them, will determine which direction our impact takes. If we tell them they can't succeed or have no real talent, we are a wall blocking their road to success.

When I found out that Lauren was a bit shy because of her height, I looked for ways I might convince her that being short is actually an advantage. She was a vocal performance major, so I searched for people in the world of entertainment who were her height and had become big stars. I had no problem finding lots of examples: Brenda Lee and Kristen Chenoweth, both petite, are two giants in the world of music. I introduced Lauren to their work, and from time to time I would introduce her to other stars who, though they were diminutive, looked tall in the spotlight's glow. I also offered my opinion that Lauren was lucky. In a world where almost everyone is average, she stood out. She was noticed, and being noticed meant that she had an advantage. Finally, whenever I could, I continued to find ways to praise all of her amazing qualities.

I don't know what this incredible young woman will accomplish in life, but I know for certain she has a much better chance of fully using her God-given talents if those around her pick her up rather than put her down. And I believe that we do that by putting faith into positive words that have impact.

I have watched many others use the same tactic I used with Lauren. Not only is it an easy way to encourage someone but it's a great vehicle to show your faith. Finding positive ways to build people up is really living as Christ lived.

Putting Faith into Action

1. Be a cheerleader, not a judge. If you want to lift someone up, show them their potential. Jesus

didn't lecture the woman at the well; she got that from all of the supposedly religious people around her. Instead, he found a way to identify with her. He gave her a loving formula for reaching her potential. If you want to make an impact, don't toss verbal stones. Give out bouquets instead.

2. Find role models for those you want to help. Do some homework and find examples of others who have done what the person you want to help aspires to do. Give the person some reasons to believe they can beat the odds.

3. Make sure the person you are trying to help feels as if they are important in your eyes. If you want them to listen to you, make sure they know you feel strongly about them. If you convince them that you believe they can change the world, they will probably begin to feel that way too.

4. Don't worry about whether they understand you are reaching out to them because of your faith. In time, they will wonder why you are helping them, and like the African elder, they will ask, "Is it your God who did this?" Once that door is opened, it will be easy to make your points. But live that sermon before you preach it.

5. Remember, talking to those you are trying to inspire isn't the only way of making an impact. Send letters, notes, or cards. Put together carefully worded emails. Send a text message or two. Make

sure they realize that they are never far from your mind and are always in your heart.

Catherine Booth was one of the best-educated Christians of her era. Yet mid-nineteenth-century London was hardly a place where a lady could take to the pulpits or the streets and voice her views on faith. The tiny English woman was handicapped by a religious society that believed women could not speak for or about God.

One evening Booth felt moved at the end of a sermon to address her church. No one was more shocked to see Catherine make her way down to the altar and stand behind the pulpit than her husband, William, the congregation's pastor. On that day, with just a few brief words, Catherine changed the course not just of her life but of the lives of millions. Why was she allowed to speak? Why did those who had gathered in that church show her respect even when she was breaking such a time-honored tradition? Because of the incredible faith they saw in her life. They believed she had been called to speak to them at that moment in time.

From that day forward, Catherine continued to speak out, even occasionally spending time in jail for using her voice as a trumpet for her faith. Many followed her because of the way she lived her life. Catherine didn't just vow to reach out to "the least of these"; she did it! She felt and lived a call to feed the hungry, clothe the naked, tend to the sick, visit the prisoners, and even minister to the city's many streetwalkers. And she never judged. Her efforts to live this faith led Catherine and her husband to found the Salvation Army. More than a century later, Catherine still speaks through the compassion shown by this worldwide organization. Her words had and continue to have great impact because she lived her faith each day of her life.

Many who speak about morality simply don't live it. When your life doesn't mirror your words, you will have little positive impact. So if you want to share your faith, make an effort to live a sermon each day of your life.

Prayer + Faith = Service

One of this nation's most popular restaurant chains was founded by Truett Cathy. When the small Georgian established Chick-fil-A, he felt the need to make a subtle statement of faith at the same time he introduced the world to his famous chicken sandwich. Truett quietly spoke a dynamic sermon when he closed his restaurants' doors on Sundays. When asked why he gave up so much business by not keeping his stores open seven days a week, he explained that he wanted his employees to have a day to worship with their families. His putting faith over profits caused a lot of folks to take note of what drove the successful businessman. It seemed that Truett took to heart what a famous missionary doctor had said almost a century earlier; Albert Schweitzer once told a gathering of college graduates, "I don't know what your destiny will be, but I do know that the only ones among you who will truly be happy are those who have sought and found how to serve."

It's easy to be a Christian. It's easier to go to church than it is to find excuses for not going. But living your faith every day of your life is the one sure way to impact others with the words you speak. If you want to share what's in your soul, use faith as a road map for your earthly travels. If you live as if you've put God first in your life, others will see it. If you live to lift others, your words will be lifted as well. If you follow this simple formula, your words will have a mighty impact!

Stories behind Christmas Boxed Set

Ace Collins, Bestselling Author

Since angels sang when Jesus was born, music has been as much a part of Christmas as candy canes, Christmas trees, and other beloved traditions of the season. Now you and your family can deepen your celebration of Christ's birth as you learn the stories and spiritual significance of our most cherished holiday songs and traditions.

Do you understand the meaning of "God Rest Ye Merry Gentlemen"? Why do we use red and green at Christmas? What are the origins of the Christmas tree? Do you know the unusual history behind "O Holy Night"?

Written by popular-music historian and bestselling author Ace Collins, the three books in this beautiful boxed set unlock the origins and meanings of best-loved carols, hymns, and songs. They also explain traditions as familiar yet little understood as mistletoe, ornaments, stockings, and holly. From the cloisters of fifth-century monks, to the frontlines of World War II, to Hollywood sets and Nashville recording studios, Collins takes you on a journey that will warm your heart and enrich your experience of this brightest of holiday seasons.

Softcover set: 978-0-310-28112-2

Pick up a copy today at your favorite bookstore!

Lije Evans Mysteries

Farraday Road

Ace Collins, Bestselling Author

A quiet evening ends in murder on a muddy mountain road.

Small town attorney Lije Evans and his beautiful wife, Kaitlyn, are gunned down. But the killers don't expect one of their victims to live. After burying Kaitlyn, Lije is on a mission to find her killer—and solve a mystery that has more twists and turns than an Ozark-mountain back road.

When the trail of evidence goes cold, complicated by the disappearance of the deputy who found Kaitlyn's body at the scene of the crime, Lije is driven to find out why he and his wife were hunted down and left for dead along Farraday Road. He begins his dangerous investigation with no clues and little help from the police. As he struggles to uncover evidence, will he learn the truth before the killers strike again?

Softcover: 978-0-310-27952-5

Pick up a copy today at your favorite bookstore!

Stories behind the Traditions and Songs of Easter

Ace Collins,
Bestselling Author

The treasured traditions of Easter—little bunnies, parades, new Easter outfits, sunrise services, passion plays, and more—infuse our celebration of the season with meaning and glowing memories. And in ways you may not realize, they point us to the resurrection of Christ and our hope of life beyond the grave. *Stories behind the Traditions and Songs of Easter* reveals the events and backgrounds that shaped the best-loved customs and songs of Easter, introducing you to stories you've never heard and a deeper appreciation for the holiday's familiar hallmarks.

Audio Download, Unabridged: 978-0-310-30528-6

Pick up a copy today at your favorite bookstore!